Ancient Mysteries,
Secret Societies,
and the Holy Grail

By
Oddvar Olsen

NEW PAGE BOOKS
A division of The Career Press, Inc.
Franklin Lakes, NJ

THE TEMPLAR PAPERS
EDITED BY CHRISTOPHER CAROLEI
TYPESET BY EILEEN DOW MUNSON
Cover design by Lu Rossman/Digi Dog Design NYC
Printed in the U.S.A. by Book-mart Press

Permission for the use of the artwork Salome, page 55, The Resurrection, page 60, and The Beheaded, page 115 given by Yuri Leitch. Permission for the use of the photos Wooden Black Madonna, page 76, Black Madonna with Child, page 80, Grail Knight, page 86, and Judgment, page 81 given by Ani Williams. Permission of the use of the photos Temple, Scotland, page 179, and Belfry, Temple, Scotland, page 187 given by Bob Mander. Permission for the use of the photo Canadian Templar Uniform, Circa 1862, page 211 given by Stephen Dafoe.

To order this title, please call toll-free 1-800-CAREER-1 (NJ and Canada: 201-848-0310) to order using VISA or MasterCard, or for further information on books from Career Press.

The Career Press, Inc., 3 Tice Road, PO Box 687,
Franklin Lakes, NJ 07417
www.careerpress.com
www.newpagebooks.com

Library of Congress Cataloging-in-Publication Data

Olsen, Oddvar, 1971-
   The Templar papers : ancient mysteries, secret societies, and the Holy Grail / by Oddvar Olsen.
      p. cm.
   Includes bibliographical references and index.
   ISBN-13: 978-1-56414-863-6
   ISBN-10: 1-56414-863-6 (pbk.)
      1. Templars—History. 2. Grail. 3. Freemasons—History. I. Title.

CR4743.O47 2006
271'.7913—dc22

2005056733

Acknowledgments

This book would not have been conceived without the articles contributed for publication in *The Temple* magazine, so a special thanks goes to all the contributors!

My biggest thanks go to my son Solomon for completing the picture. In addition, thank you to Lynne Adams, Paul Broadhurst, Gabrielle, Serena, Stephen Andrews, and Karen Ralls for continuous support and inspiration.

To Mark McGiveron, thank you for all of those long Holy Grail/ Joseph of Ariamathea/Templar conversations. To Natasha (at Chalice Well), Jamie (at Gothic Image), and Karsten (at Watkins Books), thanks for being the first bookshops that had faith in *The Temple*—without you this book may never have been published.

I'm also indebted to the staff at Wells Library, the Taunton Record Office, The British Library, and British Museum for their expertise and help in locating rare texts. Thanks to Tony and the rest of the staff at PPL.

To all the Church Wardens and key holders of the various Templar sites who have showed me around and unlocked locked doors, a similar nod of appreciation!

To the Templar spirit, Henry de Blois, and John Arthur, thank you for being beacons past and present. I have a lot of gratitude for everyone that I have met on this fabulous journey, far too many to be mentioned individually by name here. Thanks for all those illuminating discussions; all being well we will meet again soon.

Thanks to Umberto Eco, for his insight, wit, and luminous writings.

And last, but not least, I am also very grateful to everybody at Career Press and New Page Books for both approaching me to publish this compilation, and for the guidance and support that have made it what it is!

Contents

Foreword

By Dr. Karen Ralls

The memory of the Knights Templar lives on today—a historical enigma, long shrouded in mystery.

On the one hand, the Templars were known as the devout, loyal, and famed monastic warriors of the Crusades—the "white knights" of medieval Christendom. They were gifted diplomats, skillful farmers and navigators, and they established the largest multinational corporation in western Europe at the time (serving as bankers to kings, among others).

On the other hand, the Templars were rumored to have conducted mystical religious rites, guarded the Holy Grail, and possessed the lost treasures of the temple of Jerusalem.

But what is fact and what is fiction? When it comes to the Templars, this has always been the "big question." Even so, it is not always appreciated that during the time of the Templars (1119–1312), the "history" and "myths" concerning the Order were *already* becoming intertwined.

Legendary accounts of the crusades, and the Order's miraculous feats, occasionally made the rounds. For example, one such tale of the Templar's victorious battle in the holy land claimed that they may have found the gold of Solomon's Temple, the Ark of the Covenant, or ancient scrolls and relics. While some scoffed at such "nonsense," others prayed fervently for the Order to return and redeem the world after its gruelling trial and suppression.

Rumors abounded, as the shock of the Templar's demise set in (especially following the fall of Acre in 1291). After all, how could the most successful, wealthiest Order in all of Christendom come to such a brutal end, many wondered—unless the Templars had somehow lost "God's blessing"?

But with the tragic loss of the central Templar archive, the earlier factual history of the Order remains plagued with uncertainty (stemming from the lack of evidence), and so, now, as then, speculation is rife.

Written about in books old and new, this extraordinary Order has many dimensions and facets to its history—some purely historical, some more speculative. With *The Templar Papers*, British researcher and editor Oddvar Olsen has compiled selected articles from the first six issues of his magazine, *The Temple*.

Olsen's collection sheds new light on legendary events, such as the fall of Acre, as well as the history of St. Michael's Church in Garway. In addition, more speculative questions are considered, such as whether or not the Templars "head worshippers." Two key articles on the history of Freemasonry bring a valuable additional to this book. By combining the factual with the speculative, Olsen has compiled a multi-dimensional work.

I first met Olsen in the west country of England in 2002, after I had given a series of talks about medieval subjects such as the Rosslyn Chapel, Templar sites, and Grail legends to an antiquarian audience (and, on a separate evening in central Glastonbury, presented an illustrated slide lecture about the medieval Knights Templar) based on my book *The Templars and the Grail*. The next day, Olsen happened to be having lunch at the same cafe in Glastonbury, and we ended up discussing our mutual interest in the Knights Templar. At that point, *The Temple* magazine was in its early stages.

As an academic, it was truly wonderful, if not refreshing, to meet such an enthusiastic and sincere researcher with a genuine passion for his work, and the dedication to start a magazine from scratch. To see the development of this effort is pleasing indeed.

The Templars continue to fascinate us as never before, not only because of the known facts of their history, but also, with their enduring "mythos." Try as we might, the "mythos" of the Templars just won't go away. Some 800 years after their 12th-century founding, we still see them featured in many best-selling alternative history books, such as *Holy Blood, Holy Grail*, and novels such as *The Da Vinci Code*.

As a medieval historian and former Deputy Curator of a private museum exhibition on display at Rosslyn Chapel—the location of one of the key scenes in *The Da Vinci Code*—I can well attest to the growing interest not only in Rosslyn, but also in the Knights Templar.

As with the warriors of the film *Highlander*, who live forever—the memory of the Knights Templar lives on. May these selections from *The Temple* magazine, varied as they are, enrich our understanding and our Quest.

Dr. Karen Ralls

Oxford, England

November 28, 2005

www.ancientquest.com

Preface

The first issue of *The Temple* was published in August 2002, in hopes of providing a forum for authors and researchers to publish their findings. A unique selection of articles reached print in the first six issues, and in *The Templar Papers* you will find a hardy sampling of them.

In recent times, a great many books have been written about the Templar Knights. These can, in essence, be divided into two categories: the historical approach, and the legendary approach. In this volume, both perspectives have been considered.

And although the Knights Templar comprise the core of this book, to isolate the Order in history creates nothing but an unjust and inadequate picture. Subjects such as the Holy Grail legends, Arthurian mythos, the Rosicrucians, the Cathars, Gnostic theology, Rennes Le Chateau, geomancy, mythology, and symbolism are all so interrelated within the comprehensive study of the Templars that they should not be ignored.

The study of the Templars is far from an easy undertaking—we are mainly dealing with events from nearly a millennium ago, at a time when religion was at the heart of humanity. This is very different from the world in which most people now live. Consulting the medieval chroniclers is also challenging, as the style of writing was very different from today.

Throughout history, most researchers have considered the Archbishop of Acre, William of Tyre, the most reliable source of information on the foundation of the Knights Templar. His book, *The History of the Deeds Beyond the Sea*, is a momentous work on the history of the Kingdom of Jerusalem up to 1180s A.D., and is credited as the most historically reliable work of that time. (It is a truly informative and delightful read, but it is not a history book, as we know it today!) Undoubtedly, it contains many facts, but at times William was not afraid to emphasize his views on events and characters. I think it is important for today's researcher to be aware of this epical and fabled form of recording historical accounts in those bygone times (as this then invites the study of the legends and myths of that time as well). By considering all of these aspects, I hope this book will provide a more comprehensive picture of the events and individuals under investigation.

In regard to William, however, he does not mention the Templars very often in his 1,200 page book. Still, he is the primary source of information on the foundation of the Order. Most modern authors quote William in giving the full title of this newly formed order as "The Poor Knights of Christ and of the Temple of Solomon." Relying only on modern authors may sometimes be misleading, because this quotation is utterly wrong! In Volume I of *The History of the Deeds Beyond the Sea* William clearly names the order as the "Brethren of the Soldiery of the Temple, because, as we have said, they had their residence in the royal palace near the Temple of the Lord." (Throughout *The Templar Papers*, this order is generally referred to as the Knights Templar.)

Now, in regard to this compilation, having included so many different authors, I hope to have presented a comprehensive study of the Templar legacy. In some instances repetition may be found, but I felt it just to include each article in full with respect to the author's original work. However, I hope the diversity that is presented here will bring you closer to understanding the essence of the Knights Templar legacy. Some of the theories herein presented may invite further research, and some may seem controversial. Others still may answer your particular questions, while others might offer insight into subjects that have been completely overlooked in previous books written about the Templars! (Supplementary articles can be found on *The Temple* Website: *www.thetemplebooklet.co.uk*.)

The Historical Beginnings of a Knightly Order

A Brief History of the Knights Templar
By Oddbar Olsen

According to William of Tyre, the Knights Templar, or the "Brethren of the Soldiery of the Temple," as he named them, was founded in 1118 A.D.

Foremost among the nine founding knights were the venerable Hugh de Payen, (a vassal of Hugh de Champagne) and Godfrey de St. Omer. The other seven knights included Andre de Montbard (the uncle of Bernard of Clairvaux), Payen de Montdidier, Achambaud de St. Amand, Geoffroi Bisol, and Godfroi de Bouillon. All were from noble families in France, and the ruling houses in Flanders. Gondemare and Rosal also joined from the Cistercian Order of St. Bernard.

When they arrived in the Holy Land, they presented themselves to the younger brother of Godfroi de Bouillon (who had accepted the title King Baldwin II of Jerusalem), who provided the newly founded Order with quarters connected with the Al-Aqsa Mosque (which was located on the site of the famed stables at King Solomon's Temple. The Templar's mission, as stated in William of Tyre's *A History of Deeds Beyond the Sea* was: "…to keep roads and highways safe…with a special regard for the protection of pilgrims…."

"Admission of a Novice to the Vows of the Order of the Temple." From The Knights Templar, *by Robert Macoy, Masonic Publishing Company, New York, 1874.*

In 1128, at the Council of Troyes, in Champagne, France, the Knights Templar were recognized by St. Bernard of Clairvaux, and granted its "Rule of the Knights Templar." The rule gave them legal autonomy, and they would from this point forward only have to answer to the Pope and God alone.

The Pope gave his official approval of the Order in 1139, in the "Omne Datum Optimum." From that time forward the knights were granted land, castles, and economic support from kings, princes, and other noble men—not only in France, but throughout the whole of the Christianized Europe.

Having taken vows of chastity, poverty, and selfless dedication, the monastic lives of the Knights Templar was structured with rigid discipline and routine. Every aspect of their lives was decided by the regulations of Cistercian principles. For example, the knights wore their hair short, and were required to grow beards. They dressed in a simple habit of either white (for a knight, to symbolize pureness) or brown (for lesser brothers).

Additional regulations were added later. For example, in 1146 Pope Eugenius decreed that the Templar knights should wear a red cross (the Cross Patee) on their left breast. A cord was also to be worn around the waist, to remind them of their vow of chastity.

By the late 13th century, the Templars had at least 870 castles, preceptories, and subsidiary houses throughout Latin Christendom. The Order acquired some of its wealth from the protection it offered various nobles. Additionally, the knights developed the first credit note. So, instead of carrying large sums of money, for fear of robbery, one could deposit money at one preceptory, and withdraw it from another. Not only did the wealthy pilgrims take advantage of this safety, but the members of the church, nobles, and kings did so as well.

The Knights Templar used their wisdom and skills to build many of the magnificent Gothic Cathedrals. The Order's knowledge of sacred geometry and symbolism can be seen in Chartres, Notre Dame, and other architectural wonders. In addition, the influential design of the Holy Sepulcher (in Jerusalem) can be seen in the classic round Templar churches, founded on octagonal geometry.

However, the Templar's days of glory were numbered. In 1187, the great Muslim warrior Saladin recaptured Jerusalem. Even though a succession of new crusades were launched, the Christians never reclaimed control of Jerusalem. With the fall of Acre (1219), the Templar's last stronghold in the Holy Land, it appears as if the Knights Templar changed their mission.

So, what did the Knights Templar do in the Holy Land? And how good was the protection that these nine knights could offer to the perilous pilgrim routes? Very challenging questions indeed. Unfortunately, the Templar were not great writers, so few written records remain (in fact, only a few scattered accounts survive, and they mainly deal with transactions of land and properties). A few texts by contemporary writers have survived, but these mainly deal with the involvement of the Templar in various battles in the Holy Land.

The nine founding knights, with their mission to keep roads and highways safe (with a special regard for the protection of pilgrims) had very honorable intentions. Still, nine knights, however brave and advanced in warfare, would not have survived very long in combat against thousands of Christian-hating Saracens!

What we do know is that the Templar knights completed some excavations beneath Solomon's Temple. During the excavations of 1867 (by Lieutenant Warren of the Royal Engineers) various discoveries were recorded, including that of a spur, remnants of a lance, a Templar cross, and the major part of a Templar sword.

Claims have also been made that the Templar were in possession of the "Copper Scroll" (one of the Dead Sea Scrolls) discovered at Qumran. The Copper Scroll lists the burial places for the treasures of Solomon's Temple. Did the Templar find any treasures, and was this their raison d'etre?

One year before the prosecution of the Knights Templar, King Phillip le Bel of France wanted to join the order, but the Knights Templar bluntly refused him as a member. By this time, the king owed the Order a large sum of money. The suppression of the Order was about to begin. Rumors claimed that the Knights Templar held black masses at midnight, worshiped a mysterious bearded head, and defiled the cross. The long list of accusations helped the king in his opposition against the order.

On Friday the 13th, October 1307, the Grand Master Jacques de Molay and 60 other Knights Templar were captured and imprisoned in Paris, along with another 15,000 members in France. For several years, the captives were tortured. Many believe this is the reason why Friday the 13th is considered an unlucky day.

On March 14, 1314, Jaques de Molay and Geoffroy de Charney were burnt on a slow fire on the isle of Javiaux (not far from the Notre Dame in Paris). Before his death, Jaques de Molay was recorded to have prophesized the imminent demise of the king and the Pope. Both died within a year.

Was this the end of the Templar? As many volumes have already been dedicated to the history of the Knights Templar, I have only given a very brief summary for the benefit of the reader new to this subject. Instead of being repetitive, we shall, in the following pages, dwell into various aspects of Templar legacy that have not yet been dealt with sufficiently. For example, did the Templar survive after 1314?

In addition, a great many fantastic claims have been made about the Templar Order. Some of these claims are dark and disturbing, such as one that stated the Templar were devil worshippers and venerated a mysterious head! Was this the head of St. John the Baptist? Other questions relate to what the Templar knights found while excavating under the fabled Solomon's Temple. Is there any truth in that they possessed the Holy Grail, and perhaps the Ark of the Covenant? Did Freemasonry originate from the Templar? What was their relation to Mary Magdalene?

Though some of these questions may go forever unanswered, through the continuing work of scholars, some of the mysteries could some day be revealed. And regardless, the continuing interest in researching the hidden mysteries of the Knights Templar will likely keep their legacy alive in the hearts and minds of the curious.

Godfrey de Bouillon and the Early Knights Templar

The First Templars
By Sandy Hamblett

The Templar origins as a whole are completely shrouded in mystery. Not much is known about the founding Knights, and what we do know is rather vague.

Malcolm Barber and Keith Bate were probably correct when they highlighted the difference between the origins of the Knights Templar, and the demise of the Order. As they state, in *The Templars: Selected Sources*: "There is a great contrast between the obscurity of Templar origins, and the massive publicity given to their shocking demise." Why should there be such a vast difference in the "origins" of the Templars, and in their ending, with relation to historical documentation?

Some historians would probably posit that when Hugh de Payns and Godfrey de Saint-Omer approached Baldwin I they barely had an idea about the Order they wanted to inaugurate. They wanted, as is often reported, to create an order that would help protect pilgrims while visiting Jerusalem.

But are we really to believe that Hugh and his eight other companions spontaneously decided to carry out this venture? If not, when and how did they arrive at this decision? Indeed, why did they take up this risky undertaking?

It has been noted that Baldwin I, King of Jerusalem, agreed to the Templar's requests, and granted them the Al Aqsa Mosque as their residence. One might wonder, in the light of the previously mentioned facts, why a King of Jerusalem agreed to the requests of nine rather obscure knights, and gave them such illustrious headquarters. Some sources claim that it was Hugh de Payns—known as a "minor" noble from Champagne—who approached Baldwin. But this is all that is known about de Payns, and that is more than we know about the other founding knights!

It is also said that the Knights Templar, as they became known, were also protectors of the Holy Sepulcher of Christ in Jerusalem. A reason why the Templar origins might be shrouded in mystery may be because their activities of the first nine years were secret, and were meant to remain that way.

I have suggested in the past that the Knights Templar actually originated about 20 years before Hugh and his knights ever approached Baldwin I. These ideas have been expressed in various ways, most notably through the suggestion that behind the Knights Templar was a "secret society." This is not necessarily as far fetched as it seems. The aims and activities of the early knights probably attest to some sort of cohesive organization that directed those activities. There may not have been anything "sinister" in this "secret society" (different from the way in which our modern culture equates a "secret society" with all kinds of conspiracies).

Some commentators on this issue include "occult" historians, such as Arthur Waite and Albert Mackey. Waite refers to a group of individuals behind the Templars who were "magical adepts." Waite actually cites Mackey—a noted historian of Freemasonry—who states that the Rose Cross degrees in Freemasonry were instigated by Godfrey de Bouillon in Palestine, in 1100.

Even in the famous Grail literature (especially *Parsifal*, by Wolfram Von Eschenbach), one can see two levels of Templar Knights. Eschenbach distinguishes between the regular Templar Knights (the warrior monks), and the Templeis (who allegedly guarded the Grail). The Templeis are described as very spiritual, and are symbolized by the sign of the dove.

The patron saint of the Templeis appears to have been St. Odilia. Reports have documented Odilia has having lived between the fifth and sixth centuries, and her mother was called Bereswinde. Odilia's mother was the grandchild of Dagobert I, and indeed she was a sister of Dagobert II. Here we may be seeing vestiges of the Grail guardianship, as associated with the Knights Templar and the family of the Merovingians.

In books such as *Holy Blood, Holy Grail*, by Michael Baigent, et al, the heady mix of the legend swirling about the Templars, the Grail, and the Merovingians have caused much controversy. And although I do not want to go into the relative merits of these types of books, one important point to keep in mind is that Godfrey de Bouillon was of Merovingian descent on his mother's side (Ida of Lorraine).

As mentioned earlier, Mackey suggests that Godfrey had set up a group in Palestine in 1100. Waite adds that this group came to Europe in 1188, after the "troubles in Palestine."

Guillaume de Tyre claimed that the Templars were formed by nine French knights in 1118. But the fairly damning evidence that Baigent, et al, offer (in *Holy Blood, Holy Grail*) regarding the date of the Templars' creation, and the policy of those early Templars in admitting new members, convinces me that Guillaume was wrong in his date of 1118. The actual date of Templar creation seems more likely to have been around 1111.

In support of this claim, I cite the major piece of evidence concerning the Count of Anjou's joining of the Order (which is on record as having taken place in 1120). If the Order admitted no new members for its first nine years of existence, then the admission of the Count in 1120 means that the Templars were created at least by 1111. In fact, earlier dates for the creation of the Templars have been given. For example, between 1135 and 1140, Simon, a monk of St. Bertin of Sith, dated this event as 1099 (shortly after the crusades). A bishop named Anselm (of Havellburg), also wrote in 1145 about the Templar's origins, suggesting the same date of 1099.

In addition to the well-known accounts of the Templar origins given by the likes of Guillaume de Tyre, there is also another obscure account that gives details of the Templar's origins, and which has been overlooked by many historians. This is the account given by an individual known as Bernard the Treasurer. Bernard was a monk of Corbie, and his account appears to have been copied from an earlier source. (This early account has been tentatively identified as that of Ernoul. He was a servant of Balian d'Ibelin in 1187. Although Ernoul was not a living witness of the events he described, he too seems to have relied on a much earlier source for his account.)

Some neo-Templar orders exist today, and give differing histories of the founding Templars. For example, the "Chevaliers de l'ordre Notre Dame de Sion" claim the knights Templar were founded in the Holy Land in 1099 by Godfrey de Bouillon and Brother Hugh de Payn s (Count of Champagne). In fact, they claim a heritage from the Knights Templar. But in their account, Godfrey de Bouillon is cited as a founder!

So, we have reoccurring, but contradictory, dates and names in relation to the formation of the Knights Templar. We have 1099, 1111, and 1118. The common thread in this confusion always appears to be Godfrey de Bouillon. So, why is there so much confusion regarding this subject?

Was de Bouillon responsible for setting up an order after he conquered the Holy Land and reclaimed the Holy Sepulcher from the infidels?

There does appear to have been a "real" Order set up by Godfrey in the Holy Land (The Order of the Holy Sepulcher). Apparently he gathered around him 12 Knights—and these Knights were to protect the religious chapter of canons, who were serving at the Sepulcher of Christ when Godfrey and his army arrived.

Many commentators are prepared to accept that Godfrey established the Order of the Holy Sepulcher. All agree that there was a religious order (the canons of the Holy Sepulcher) under the rule of Saint Augustine, and who were to be protected by the new knights (led by Godfrey). The canons are never, at any time, said to have been military in nature. It is interesting to note here, however, that these canons do appear to have been involved in one way or another with the military orders, and also with individuals trying to protect pilgrims and the Holy Sepulcher. For example, a knight named Paganus managed to obtain a hall from these canons of the Temple of the Lord, so that he could recruit more men from among visiting knights. These canons at the temple and the Holy Sepulcher are said to have worked together.

Godfrey supposedly established his Order in 1099, and it makes sense that it was an Order of the Holy Sepulcher, for this is what the Crusades were, in part, concerned with. These knights, therefore, intended to protect the Christian presence at the Sepulcher for 20 years. And then, in 1122 Pope Callistus issued a Bull. They then became a "lay religious community" who were to guard the Sepulcher and the city of Jerusalem. Based on this evidence, I believe the Order was first established about 1100—pretty close to the previously given date of 1099.

Once Godfrey had liberated the Holy Sepulcher, he set up residence on Mount Sion, within the walls of the Tower of David. In fact, recent research has suggested that the origins of the Temple can be found in the associations that the knights formed with the canons of the Holy Sepulcher, and that in 1120 they had received permission to form a separate group. Some other researchers have made a direct link between de Bouillon, his clerics and canons, and the Holy Sepulcher. It seems this group may have been known as the "Milites Christi," or "Milites Sancti Sepulchri." It has been suggested that some "westerners" (Godfrey's retinue?) broke away from the Holy Sepulcher to form a military order. Bernard the Treasurer has no hesitation in identifying these persons as the earliest Templars. Bernard even refers to these knights as having worn the Red Cross insignia (similar to that of the Holy Sepulcher).

It is my contention that Godfrey, once he had liberated the Holy Sepulcher, installed his knights (as well as his canons) into the Holy Sepulcher—this is a matter of historical record—as a military presence. Approximately 20 years later, the Knights Templar arose from this group. This theory gains support when we consider that Bernard the Treasurer's account of the formation of the Templars did not ascribe any initiative on the part of Hughes de Payns. Bernard also did not refer to any alleged reason the Templars were formed—that being to protect pilgrims.

It is Bernard who emphasized the Templars connection with the Holy Sepulcher. The connections include the facts that the Templars' liturgy was that of the Holy Sepulcher, that the "French rule" (dating to 1140) stated that it was "l'ordinaire del Sepulchre," and that the peculiar way that Templars built their churches—which were often polygonal—was inspired by the Church of the Holy Sepulcher.

An 18th century theologian, Johann August Starck, suggested that the Templars eventually were able to appoint their own priests, and that they did this with the permission of the Pope. Starck asserted that these priests were the "inner order" of the Knights Templar, and that they were "directly descended from the Canons of the Holy Sepulcher." It is interesting that an 18th century theologian should have the same information that modern historians are just now coming to realize and identify! It is my contention that the nobility and knights who accompanied Godfrey were the same knights he gathered around him at the Holy Sepulcher. The priests who came with him—and were later installed in the Holy Sepulcher—probably constituted the real "inner order" (or founders) of the Knights Templar.

I have only read about the alleged connection of the Templars with the Holy Sepulcher and Godfrey within the confines of Château (specifically in the works of Deloux and Bretigny). It is interesting that modern research may be indicating the same ideas.

The connections between these people and Godfrey happen to be through blood ties, and here, we might note that Godfrey was elected "Ruler of Jerusalem," and, in all but name, was the King of Jerusalem (because he was of the sacred line of the Merovingians). The founding Templars were likely obedient to, and probably worked with, Godfrey. He is known to have made his base at the Tower of David, on Mount Sion. Godfrey built an abbey there, and then fortified the existing structures.

You may feel that all these ideas regarding the secrecy surrounding Godfrey, and his setting up of an Order, may fall into the realms of fantasy.

If so, I must refer you to a historian and contemporary of the first crusaders, Albert of Aachen. On several occasions, he describes a group called the domus Godefridi, clientele Godefridi, or domus ducis. As Alan Murray suggests in *The Crusader Kingdom of Jerusalem*, "this term may have referred to Godfrey's immediate retinue rather than the entirety of the Frankish forces."

The members of this group appear to have constituted the key personnel through which Godfrey's rule functioned. They were also instrumental in the accession of his brother, Baldwin I (which is interesting considering that it was this Baldwin who later gave the Templars their headquarters—perhaps he was just carrying out Godfrey's plans). The *domus Godefridi* appear to have been obscure in origin—almost as obscure as Hugh de Payns himself. Albert of Aachen does, however, name (and provide information about) the composition of some of this group. According to Albert, the group included higher clergymen. There were also important Lotharingian men in this group, and some would appear to be members related to Godfrey—if not blood relatives, still close associates—likely from the domains that he held in Lotharingia (the old name for Lorraine).

I suggest that the canons and knights instituted by Godfrey later became the Knights Templar. Knowledge of the Order was probably held within the nobility and family members. When Bernard of Clairvaux championed the sanction and rule of the Templars, there were already family members from Champagne/Burgundy, and the territories of de Bouillon's birthplace, within the ranks of the Templars.

Is it possible that the known historical founders of the Templars became allied to these early Templars through family associations and knowledge that was handed down? If this was the case, then they may have appeared as founders of the Order, when in actuality they were just carrying out plans begun by Godfrey de Bouillon some 20 years earlier.

Godfrey de Bouillon's Templar Knights, Mount Sion, and the Essenes
By Sandy Hamblett

The major crusader knight associated with many events in Palestine at the time of the first crusade was Godfrey de Bouillon. Godfrey, as we know, was of Merovingian descent on his mother's side. Given the legends surrounding the Merovingian bloodline, I wondered if Godfrey may have had an ulterior motive when he marched on Jerusalem in 1099.

When the crusaders finally liberated the Holy Sepulcher (the supposed reason for the Pope's calling for the crusades) Godfrey was elected as "King of Jerusalem." Godfrey declined this office, and instead accepted the title of "Protector of the Holy Sepulcher." The anonymous conclave of individuals who made this decision to vote for Godfrey have eluded all historical enquiry regarding their identity. That is, until recently. In my article, "The First Templars," I pointed out the overwhelming evidence suggesting that the Templar Knights were instigated by Godfrey de Bouillon and his association with the Holy Sepulcher.

An eyewitness of the first crusade, and indeed, the "official biographer" of Godfrey, was a man named Albert of Aachen. Albert discussed the "domus godefridi" (a body of men with whom Godfrey was able to rule Jerusalem). I think this group was the anonymous conclave that carried out political will at the time of the first crusade. Most of this conclave I am going to term "the Lorraine Fraternity"—after Butler and Dafoe (who also discuss a secret conclave of individuals whom they term the Troyes Fraternity), who discuss the individuals who "kept" Godfrey, and later, his brother Baldwin I, in power. These appear to be blood relatives of the Merovingians, or were persons who held very high places back in the land of Godfrey's before he left for the Holy Land.

It is after the capture of the Holy Land that the Knights Templar are said to have formed. The Knights Templar later became synonymous with the idea of the warrior monks protecting pilgrims—this may have an element of truth on some level—but this reason may have been confused with an allied aim (that after Jerusalem was conquered, the holy places had to then be protected from falling back into Muslim hands). It is easy to see why this aim would have later become synonymous with pilgrim protection.

But in Godfrey's time, not only do his Templars not seem to have taken this form, the official historical date of the Templar's formation is given as about 1118. (This can be dismissed when looking at other contemporary documentation regarding why the Templars were formed, as opposed to the continual references to William of Tyre—indeed on several occasions it can be shown that this chronicler is wrong in his date for the formation of the Templars.)

According to Dominic Selwood, the fact that Count Fulk of Anjou became a "confrater" of the Templars between 1120 and 1121 suggests that this is one year after the foundation of the Order, whereas William of Tyre says no new members were admitted to the ranks of the Templars for nine years after their foundation. Is the date of creation then somewhere between 1111 and 1112?

The only group that Godfrey appears to have been connected with was the one he set up called the "Order of the Holy Sepulcher." This sounds plausible. If he was in fact the "Protector of the Holy Sepulcher" it is highly probable that Godfrey installed a knightly order to protect the very Sepulcher he sought to liberate.

There are suggestions by various "occult" historians that Godfrey did set up a society, that appeared to be related to, but not exactly, the Knights of the Holy Sepulcher. For example, Albert Mackey asserts that Godfrey set up a society in Palestine in 1100 (whose emblems were the rose and cross, inferring that one should see in this group the origins of the Rosicrucians). Modern historians are just beginning to see the connections of Godfrey, the Holy Sepulcher, and the Templars.

Godfrey only lived for one year after his capture of Jerusalem, with some historians suggesting he had been poisoned. For example, see the accounts of Mathew of Edessa, an Armenian chronicler, who reports:

> In 1100 Godfrey, leader of the Franks, came with his army to Caesarea of Philippi…the Muslim leaders went to meet him on the pretext of making peace: they bought supplies and served them in his presence. Godfrey accepted and unsuspectingly ate the dishes they presented, which were poisoned. He died several days later along with forty other people.

So, maybe Godfrey did establish an Order on his deathbed. As Godfrey's brother Baldwin then took the title "King of Jerusalem," perhaps the Order was entrusted to Baldwin? If so, this would be significant, because Baldwin I later gave the Knights Templar their headquarters on the Temple Mount.

Godfrey's "rose and cross" society might in some way correlate with information also supplied by Waite. He refers to a "Society of Ormus," who claimed that they were the founders of the Rosicrucian Order. Waite tells us that this "Ormus" Order had close links with the Knights Templar, and it may be that Mackey and Waite are both reporting the same information, but from different sources.

There is enough overlap in their separate accounts to suggest this. For example, Waite's "Society of Ormus" came to Europe in 1188—which he confirms was an important date for the Knights Templar. (Historical records document that up until this time the Priory of Sion and the Knights Templar shared the same Grand Master. The Priory of Sion were said to be a secret society behind the Templars—and also behind the election of Godfrey as well—who also used the subtitle of Ormus. In their literature, this group asserted that an important date for them was 1188. This is when they separated from the Knights Templar and went their own way (in what is often referred to as the "Splitting of the Elm.") This would suggest that the Order of Sion, which claimed to have been created by Godfrey de Bouillon, was analogous to the "Lorraine Fraternity."

Thus there does seem to be circumstantial evidence that Godfrey did indeed set up a knightly order in the Holy Land. And from most reports, the reoccurring themes seem to be that the order was secretive, hermetical, and alchemical, connected very closely with the Knights Templar, and that Godfrey de Bouillon was the founder. The idea of secrecy may not imply any sinister intent. However, it may indicate a "plan of action," on the part of Godfrey and this "Lorraine Fraternity." This plan of action would seem to involve France, the Holy Land, the Templars, and, of course, the Lorraine Fraternity.

This is not as wild an idea as it seems. Jean Markale, in *The Templar Treasure at Gisor*, makes mention of a letter written by a very famous monk named Gerbert of Aurillac (who later became Pope Sylvester II). This Pope had (some 100 years before the first crusade) suggested in a letter that he "hopes France would recover the holy places so that a search could be made for the keys to the Universal Understanding hidden there." This of course suggests that knowledge of some sort was known, and that it would necessitate a search of the Holy Places.

There is evidence that the Templars, and by association the Knights and monks installed by Godfrey de Bouillon (and even Godfrey himself), did undertake various searches among the Holy Places. This secret society of proto-Templars—and in particular—the "secret order" behind them (whether the Order of Sion, or whether an inner group of Godfrey's), were said to have occupied the Abbey of Notre Dame du Mont de Sion until 1187.

Godfrey de Bouillon did set up residence at Mount Sion after his liberation of the Holy Sepulcher. The Abbey on Mount Sion included the Tomb of David, the Cenacle, and the ancient Church of the Apostles. The site has been regularly excavated since at least the 1970s, and if one considers the discoveries found on the site, it might help us to better understand the motives of Godfrey de Bouillon and those associated with him.

A major discovery is the identification of this site with an ancient Essene community who lived here during the time of Jesus. The Essenes are identified as those priests and monks who lived a sectarian existence (along the shores of the Dead Sea, and other places), and who are generally accepted as the creators of the Dead Sea Scrolls. These facts have the ability to bring into focus a hypothesis about what Godfrey, in the vein of Pope Sylvester's II letter suggests, may have discovered in his journeys.

Another amazing discovery I have uncovered while researching was the fact that medieval copies of Qumran documents exist. These include two fragments of the manuscript found at Qumran (later called the Damascus Document). They have been dated as originating some time between the 10th and 12th centuries, respectively. How can it be that copies of Scrolls, dating to the Middle Ages, were found before the discovery of the Dead Sea Scrolls in 1947? Remember, the existence of the Scrolls was not even known of until their discovery. Could there be some link with Godfrey, the Essene settlement at Mount Sion (where he built the abbey), and the medieval copies of the Dead Sea Scrolls? Could this information help us to understand how the Templars later had an aura of mystery surrounding them, and why the Templars began to appoint their own priests, conduct secret rituals, and be reported to have held heretical beliefs about Jesus Christ? Could it suggest some solution to the "universal understanding hidden there"?

Mount Sion excavations

In *Holy Blood, Holy Grail*, the authors state that the Templars, and the secret society behind them, occupied a structure on Mount Sion that they called the Abbey of Notre Dame du Mont de Sion, and that it housed this secret society until 1187. This abbey appears to have been built over an older site (which was said to house the Tomb of David, the Cenacle, and the ancient Church of the Apostles). As this Church of the Apostles seemed to be important to the crusaders, I decided to look into its history. I was curious, for example, why this church was known as the "mother of all churches," and why Godfrey de Bouillon wanted to build an Abbey there. What exactly constituted the building works of Godfrey and his Knights? And who and what community was housed in this Abbey? Simialrly, I was curious whether there is any significance to the recent discovery that this site was also the site of an Essene settlement in Jerusalem?

Remember, the Mount Sion we are discussing is the hill that sits to the west of the Tyropoeon Valley. (Sion is also the name given to the old "City of David," and to the Temple Mount in Jerusalem.) Here, on the western side of Mount Sion, is the site of a very ancient church—called the Church of the Apostles. Jacob Pinkerfeld excavated this site and suggested that the foundation floor could be evidence of a Judeo-Christian synagogue—which he assumed had been built by the first "Christians."

When the crusaders arrived, they began to build on this site at Mount Sion, supporting the assertions made by Baignet and others. The crusaders indeed added to the building of this Church of the Apostles. (The archaeological evidence for this includes eight crusader-pillar foundations, and some rooms and designs that the crusaders added to the basic structure.) For example, the crusaders built the Chapel of the Holy Spirit, which commemorated the appearance of the Holy Spirit to the disciples. They also decorated the Cenotaph of David with rosettes, and they built a room called the Chamber of Mysteries—a most suggestive title.

The Chamber of Mysteries was built over the Cenacle—and it is this room that is associated with the Last Supper. The crusaders also carved grapes onto the pillars—a symbol of the wine used at the Eucharist. Although, it has also been suggested that the grapes may have other symbolism (Jesus himself is said to have referred to grapes, vines, and viticulture—perhaps suggesting his Davidic bloodline). These symbols were found within the room of the Cenacle. Perhaps it was here in the Chamber of Mysteries that the early Templars held their first rituals.

The Abbey de Notre Dame du Mont de Sion

Lincoln, et al (1996) refer to "numerous extant charters, chronicles, and contemporary accounts" that suggest an abbey was built on these Byzantine ruins. They suggest that the abbey was built at the behest of Godfrey de Bouillon (although they do not appear to cite their sources for this).

Even though Godfrey was building an abbey, Lincoln reports that:

> ...one chronicler, writing in 1172, recorded that this construction of Godfrey's was an "imposing edifice"—a veritable self contained community...well-fortified with

its own walls, towers, and battlements. Now, the question
that must be asked is whether this building of Godfrey's
was "just" an abbey, and what group constituted this
"veritable, self-contained community"?

Does a simple abbey need towers and battlements? Yes, perhaps, if
the community had something of value within the walls. It is also possible that the abbey needed protection from outsiders. This may well be
the case.

As we discussed, the crusaders built a room called the Chamber of
Mysteries. It is not known what took place in this room, or what was
housed in the room. It is this structure which is asserted to be the "Abbey
of Notre Dame du Mont de Sion." Archaeologists, however, have not at
any time recorded that this site was indeed called by this name.

Lincoln, et al, give us further accounts of this abbey in *Holy Blood,
Holy Grail*: "…according to the leading 19th-century expert on the sub-
ject, the abbey was inhabited by a chapter of Augustinian
Canons…charged with serving the sanctuaries under the direction of an
abbot. The community assumed the double name of "Saint Marie du
Mont Syon et du Saint Esprit."

They also report the following: "…another historian, writing in 1698,
is more explicit still: 'There were in Jerusalem…during the
crusades…knights attached to the Abbey of Notre Dame de Sion—who
took the name of Chevaliers de L'Ordre de Notre Dame de Sion.'"

In these statements it is suggested that knights were attached to the
abbey/Church of the Apostles. If Godfrey commanded the building of
this abbey, could he not have installed the Knights that this 1698 historian referred to? We know that Godfrey had done this before (when he
had installed 12 knights at the Holy Sepulcher in Jerusalem).

In my past research I have found evidence that suggests Godfrey's Knights of the Holy Sepulcher could have held within its ranks the Order of Sion (in the form of certain knightly nobles from particular families). I refer to the work of the 18th-century theologian, Johann Starck. As cited in *The Templars' Secret Island*, Starck suggested that the Templars eventually came to appoint their own priests, and that they did this with the permission of the Pope. Starck claimed that these priests were the "inner order" of the actual Knights Templar, and that they were "directly descended from the Canons of the Holy Sepulcher."

If Godfrey, and the nobility who accompanied him to the Holy Land (and later became knights), were the same knights he had gathered around him at the Holy Sepulcher, and who later went onto become the inner and upper echelons of the Knights Templar, Starck's supposition that the Templar priests were an "inner order" seems much more plausible.

Would the inner order of the Templars—who were descended from the Canons of the Holy Sepulcher—constitute the same 20 canons (and 12 Knights) that Godfrey is known to have installed at the Holy Sepulcher? And, if Godfrey installed Knights here, then couldn't he have installed knights at the Abbey he built on Mount Sion?

Let me remind you of Starck's comment, as cited in *The Templars' Secret Island*, regarding the secret group of canons: "[they were] a secret brotherhood within the brotherhood—forever united with the Templar Order."

So, if Godfrey's secret and hermetic group of Canon Knights were installed at the ancient Church of the Apostles, what else can we say about this chosen site?

What happened to the early apostles on Mount Sion?

If we consider Pinkerfeld's excavations again—particularly those of the original floor layers—we can note that he found some niches that corresponded to other early synagogues (used to store arks for the Torah scrolls). This is explained by the fact that the earliest Jewish Christians had not divorced themselves from their Judaic roots or religion. In the early years of Christianity, as Pixner and others report, there seemed to be a conflict between the Jewish Christians and the Gentile Christians. The arguments appear centered around points of doctrine, and particularly of how Paul was interpreting the life of Jesus (and what type of person he was). The Jewish Christians did not accept such doctrines as the Virgin Birth and the divinity of Jesus. The Jewish Christians called their houses of worship a "synagogue," while the Gentile Christians—wanting to distance themselves from the Jewish Christians—adopted the word "ekklesia," which later became known simply as the Church. So, this Church of the Apostles was a synagogue, and can be said to have been used by Jewish Christians.

Pixner, from his own excavations, reconstructed the history of the Church of the Apostles. He found coins dating to the First Jewish Revolt (67–68 A.D.), and concluded that the synagogue, church, and other structures were razed during this Roman attack. He found additional support for his archaeological evidence within contemporary writings of historians.

For example, Pixner cites Eusebius, a respected church historian, who wrote that the early Jewish Christians "escaped" this attack by fleeing to Pella in the Trans-Jordan. Eusebius tells us these early Christians were awaiting the return of Christ, and when this didn't occur they returned to Jerusalem and built their "sanctuary" at the site of the Last Supper on

Mount Sion. As Pixner recounts, this particular group of Christians were allowed to return after the Roman destruction of Jerusalem because the Romans recognized the validity of their religion. It was the Gentile Christians who were persecuted as being illegitimate. Their legitimacy only came hundreds of years later—when Emperor Constantine made Christianity the official state religion of Rome. By then a total and irreconcilable split had occurred between the two sets of Christians.

It is here that the details of the early church become clearer. The Gentile Christians had embraced the teachings of Paul—which allowed all non-Jews to become Christians. The Jewish Christians did not accept this at all, and, in fact, fought bitterly with the Gentile Christians. (The Jewish Christians also seem to have been known by many different names, including the Ebionites, and the Nasoreans.)

The early Jewish Christians are said to have centered around a more primitive community, based on the teachings of James ("the brother of the Lord"). Eusebius, as Pixner again furnishes for us, claimed that this flourishing Judeo-Christian community was presided over by 13 bishops from this early church. It appears that it is this synagogue and Church of the Apostles from whence the bishops came.

Another historian, Bishop Epiphanius (315–403 A.D.) records that there was on Mount Sion a small church of God. He tells us that it is marked by the Upper Room to which the disciples returned from the Mount of Olives—that can only mean the Church of the Apostles. This Church was already standing in 130 A.D., and, as Pixner tells us: "...according to Euthychius, the Judeo-Christians who fled to Pella to escape the Roman destruction in 70 A.D. returned to Jerusalem in the fourth year of the emperor Vespasian and built their church."

After the community returned to Jerusalem, they did so under the "leadership" of an individual known as Simon Bar Kleopha—who was said to be the second Bishop of Jerusalem after the death of James, the brother of Jesus. This Simon was also a descendant of the royal Davidic family.

Is Jesus' family the first community of the church of the apostles on Mount Sion?

Eusebius fills in a little more information about this Simon. He was a known brother of Joseph of Nazareth (in his "Church History")—that would make him a cousin of Jesus.

It appears then that this site on Mount Sion was frequented on many occasions by Jesus and his family members. Jesus held his Last Supper there, before he was arrested and crucified. Immediately thereafter, it seems, a Judeo-Christian group rallied—and after the destruction of the Temple in 70 A.D.—came back here to build their synagogue and church. The leader of the community was "first" James, but later, the post was filled by Simon Kleophas—who, as we have just noted, was a cousin of Jesus. Then, it appears that this Jewish community had an apostolic succession from Jesus and that the leaders of the community were chosen because they were of Jesus' bloodline.

In fact—as John the Baptist was the cousin of Jesus—it's probable that he was the leader of the community until his death, when Jesus took over. (This idea of a family continuation becomes very important later on in this article. The fact that John the Baptist is thought to have been at some time in his life a member of the Essene Community is also of paramount importance. The link becomes the possible writings of this community, Godfrey de Bouillon, and the early Templar Knights.) Or perhaps Jesus created a new "social" movement? And as these family members also seem to have been bishops of the community, perhaps Jesus sent out others to spread the "message." This could surely have been men as well as women (for example, Mary Magdalene and Mary of Bethany—depending on whether you see these as two separate people).

Some observers believe that the Merovingain dynasty of Kings—who later came to rule France—was related to this family of Jesus. We have to be quite clear about this. It is indeed possible that members of Jesus' family continued into our modern times. Although sensationally described as possibly occurring via a bloodline from Jesus and Mary Magdalene—it is not necessary for a bloodline related to Jesus to have survived in this manner.

Many early church fathers discussed the brothers and sisters of Jesus, and their survival after the death of Jesus. They also refer to active participation of Roman authorities, who wanted to eradicate the Despoysni (the term given to blood relatives of Jesus). Therefore, the Romans followed a policy "hunting out" these people and executing them. Records were also destroyed.

What was the purpose of this policy? It was to quell the continued insurrections and Jewish uprisings within Jerusalem (that eventually found their way back to this family). It is possible that Godfrey of Bouillon, who was a Merovingian descendant on his mother's side, could trace his ancestors back to Jewish roots and family members of Jesus. Is it also possible that those knights who came with Godfrey on the first crusade, along with the anonymous conclave who elected Godfrey as Protector of the Holy Sepulcher—and who later allowed his brother Baldwin to become King of Jerusalem—knew of the family connections between Godfrey (and his brother) and the Merovingains, hence the family descendants of Jesus.

Would this in fact explain the conundrum that historians often refer to? That, in the face of stiff competition, Godfrey was still elected "protector" of the Sepulcher and Jerusalem, when in fact a "better" claim was forthcoming from Raymond of Toulouse? Did Godfrey have family traditions that everyone accepted as legitimate? Was Godfrey able to support his claim on this basis?

And would not the Church of the Apostles be the obvious place for Godfrey to build his Abbey with fortified battlements? The place where Jesus seemed to virtually "live," and where a very important biblical event (the Last Supper) took place?

Was this Mount Sion community also an Essene community?

Pixner excavated the western hill of Mount Sion. In the documentation of his findings, he explained how the historian Josephus had referred to the "Gate of the Essenes," and had suggested that this gate was on Mount Sion. This inspired Pixner to search for the Essene Gate. The Essenes, of course, are now notorious as the supposed community who lived a solitary existence by the Dead Sea at Qumran. It is this group who are believed to have been the writers of the Dead Sea Scrolls found in 1947. Pixner described how he found the Essene Gate of Jerusalem. He managed to find the gate, and with it, an undisturbed archaeological layer that contained pottery shreds that dated to 70 C.E. Further excavations, along Josephus' supposed First Wall, and especially adjacent to the Essene Gate, allowed the team to excavate right down to a rock scarp. They eventually found the "inner face" of this First Wall—and calculated that the wall must have been 8 feet wide. Pottery dated this wall to between the seventh and eighth centuries C.E. (It was this wall that the Bible claimed

Hezekiah built—and once this wall was found, Pixner was able to tell how the Essene Gate was constructed. As he states:

> ...to construct the gate the builders made a breach into the existing wall. Then they dug a sewage channel...that ran along the street and emptied into the Hinnom Valley, south of Mount Sion. Limestone of fine workmanship covers the channel as it passes beneath the gateway....

Other archeological finds suggested that a "middle sill," for example, was built directly over the top of the Essene gate that: "could have been part of a gate in a makeshift wall built by the Jewish Christians who remained on Mount Sion."

Pixner notes that the Jewish Christians appear to have built a wall around their quarter and their synagogue. Because the Jewish Christians were becoming more and more distant from the Gentile Christians, he speculated that they appear to have been "shunned as heretics" by the Christians because the Jewish Christians would not accept the doctrinal decision at the Council of Nicea in 325 C.E.

As Pixner observed, city gates are usually named after the locations to which their streets lead. Hence the Damascus Gate leads to Damascus. Did the Essenes Gate lead to an Essene Quarter?

There is evidence that the Essenes lived not only at Qumran, but in other places as well (for example, Jerusalem—see the War Scroll— Josephus, Philo). The Essene Movement was apparently made up of Zadokite kohanim, or priests. They trace their ancestry back to the House of Zadok, a son of Aaron. When the Hasmonean kings took on the role of priests as well, the Essene Zadokites refused to accept this and opposed their rule (especially when it came to temple life). They therefore removed themselves from such polluted institutions.

Because the Essenes had such strict rules of purity (and did not want to mix with the heathen population), the community was expected to maintain its rigorous standards. From his archaeological excavations, Pixner furnishes much evidence to support this idea. He found ritual baths on Mount Sion, within this Essene settlement. The baths were as substantial and in the manner of those found at Qumran. When Pixner presented this evidence to a leading Israeli archaeologist, he was told: "…here you have got excellent proof that the Essenes lived in this corner of Jerusalem…."

What are we to make of this proof? Is it proof, beyond a doubt, that a substantial number of Essenes lived on Mount Sion (as termed by ancient historians the Essene Quarter), and now attested to archaeologically?

What are we to make of the fact that this is where Jesus celebrated his Last Supper with his disciples in the Essene Quarter? What are we to make of the evidence that the earliest Jerusalem church (descended from Jesus) built a synagogue over the Cenacle? What are we to make of the community of leaders and bishops of Jerusalem who appear to have been selected because of their familial relationship to Jesus? If a substantial community of strict Jewish Essenes lived on Mount Sion at the time of Jesus, and, in fact, who appear to have played host to Jesus—allowing him to commemorate his Last Supper there before his arrest, trial and crucifixion—is it not plausible to assume that Jesus had strong links with the Essene Movement? After all, it is well-known that the Qumran community had a ritual communal meal. This could indeed correlate with Jesus' Last Supper. The fact that Jesus could even move freely among this community also suggests that Jesus was accepted in the Essene Community in Jerusalem. Groups such as the Nazarenes and the Ebionites are certainly said to contain members from Jesus' family, so they could correlate with the Jewish-Christians who lived on Mount Sion.

Irenaeus tells us that these Ebionites denied the divinity of Jesus, and that they denied the Virgin Birth. They also used a Hebrew version of the Gospel of Matthew. In the battles between the Jewish-Christians and the Gentile-Christians we can see the split taking place. St. Epiphanius tells us that these Ebionites were "heretics." I suggest that they were labeled heretics because they would not accept coalescing Roman Orthodoxy. And it was these Ebionites, Epiphanius tells us, who were associated with the Essenes. Would this be the Essenes who also had their Quarter on Mount Sion?

Perhaps we should consider a group called the "Sons of the Prophets." Pliny suggested that these Sons of the Prophets stemmed directly from the Essenic tradition. The Sons of the Prophets were actually Nazirites, and had taken the Nazirite vow. Their origins coincide with Samuel, and the origins of the kingship and monarchy traditions in Israel. Other commentators, such as Basil, Gregory, and John Chrystostom, have suggested that the Sons of the Prophets were the precursors to the later hermits and monks, and that they were associated with the Essenes and the Therapeutes of Egypt. Pliny, Josephus, and Philo all agree with these assertions too.

If these assertions are accepted, then a very interesting picture develops regarding the Messiah of Israel and the rightful King of Jerusalem, as well as the events in Palestine around the time of Jesus. If, as it seems possible, that from the Sons of the Prophets came the Nazirites, did this, in turn, lead to the formation of the Essenes? Did these movements later become associated with Jesus and John the Baptist?

The famous archaeologist Yigael Yadin felt that Jesus was a leader of a "schismatic faction of the Essenes." Could this group of schismatics be the Essenes who were based on Mount Sion? Is this why Jesus could move freely amongst them? If John the Baptist was a more prophetic type of Essene (as discussed by Josephus) could Jesus have been trying something new? It is possible that when Jesus took over the "mantle" of the group (after the death of his cousin John), he tried to call Jews to God. And perhaps, after his death, other family members then replaced Jesus.

In fact, this supposition allows for another interesting sequence of events. When Jesus began preaching in Israel, it is known that John the Baptist sent some of his disciple to join his group. One of these disciples appears to include the subsequent disciple known as the "Beloved Disciple." Here we see a direct link between the Baptist, the Essenes, and the Jesus Movement, even if one did not want to accept that family relations existed.

From the Beloved Disciple, we move into Gnostic theology and the theology of the Gospel of John. This creates a whole new very interesting line of research involving the identity of the Beloved Disciple and the Johanine Communtiy. In fact, it may also shed light on why the Templars were known as the Knights of St. John, and why they were said to be "Johaninne Christians." Were the trials and tribulations of the "Movement" and of the family of King David recorded for posterity (and which came to form in the teachings of the Community)? Did the Essenes write their scrolls, and teach from the scrolls in the ways that they did—exalting their members to be staunch followers of the law of God, to oppose any usurpers, and to proclaim a new covenant? Were Jesus' Essenes reformers of the "new covenant"?

Some archaeologists believe that there was in fact a Scriptorium at Qumran—where the literate members of the community would write down, copy, and preserve ancient teachings and history. The result is the magnificent find of the Dead Sea Scrolls in 1947. From these discoveries, scholars found a huge amount of information that revolutionized speculation on the origins of Christianity.

If the Essene settlement in Jerusalem was as substantial as the community at Qumran, however, the Jerusalem Essenes could have copied scrolls and kept written histories. As yet, we cannot say this was definitely the case, for the whole of the Mount Sion area has yet to be fully excavated.

Did Godfrey go to Mount Sion for a reason?

It has been suggested that when Godfrey and his precursor Templar Knights arrived in Jerusalem, various events took place. For example, it has persistently claimed throughout history that the Templars were actively looking for something (treasure, perhaps, and other artifacts). It has also been said that they discovered the Ark of the Covenant, scrolls, and knowledge (specifically said to be the true life of Christ, and evidence that he survived the Crucifixion). When Godfrey arrived at Mount Sion and started to rebuild the abbey with fortified towers and battlements over the Church of the Apostles, he installed there his canons and knights—could they have possibly found scrolls similar to the ones at the Dead Sea?

This does not sound so far fetched. In 1897, Solomon Schechter discovered a *genizah* (a hiding place) at the Ben Ezra Synagogue in Old Cairo. (This synagogue was originally called the "Men of Israel," and was built in 882 A.D. on the remains of a Coptic church basilica previously sold to the Jews. It also became known as the synagogue of Elijah, who is said to have been a member of the "Sons of the Prophets"—the group referred to above).

Schechter found a hoard of sacred books and scrolls of the law in the Genizah. Part of the hoard consisted of medieval fragments that turned out to be copies of the Damascus Document (a Qumran sectarian work). The fragments have been dated to the 10th and 12th centuries, and the manuscripts themselves now reside at Cambridge University.

Also found with it were fragments of the Aramaic Levi and fragments of the original Hebrew of Ben Sira. It is not understood how the Damascus Document of the Qumran Community could have ended up in Cairo. However, two theories have been put forward. Speaking at a lecture on the Demascus Document and community rule, James R. Devila stated the following:

> [It is possible the documents] have been copied in an unbroken manuscript tradition in Jewish circles into the Middle Ages, or that they may have been recovered during the early middle ages in caves in Palestine in discoveries like those mentioned by Origen and Timothy, and then copied and passed along, perhaps in quasi-heretical 'karaite' circles until they ended up in Egypt.

If future excavations find a scriptorium on Mount Sion, this may perhaps suggest that the Crusaders themselves found scrolls and holy books. Perhaps the canons that Godfrey installed, being priests, would have had the literary skills, and motivation, to translate or copy them. The point is that, with the existence of these medieval copies of the Dead Sea Scrolls, this idea is not as far-fetched as it seems. It is known, for example, that the Jewish communities paid the crusaders money—and substantial sums at that—for the return of their Holy Books (that the crusaders likely looted).

The genizah manuscripts preserve the following parts of the Damascus Document:

1. Admonition (this includes the origins of the movement), starting with a survey of biblical history.

2. The Laws.

3. Communal Rules.

The Community Rule describes an organization similar to that of the Essenes. It allows no free will, advocates communal ownership of property, and gives similar rules for joining the community (for example, it prescribes an oath that must be taken by members, and a common meal to be shared by all ceremonially pure members). Perhaps this was what the Essene settlement on Mount Sion was doing when the Last Supper took place?

Another possibility is that if the code that Dr. Hugh Schonfield found in some of the Dead Sea Scrolls (the "Atbash Cipher," that was later used by the Templars) could be proved to be the exact same cipher used in both instances, it is possible that the Templars did get access to some of the Dead Sea Scrolls before modern humanity ever knew of their existence. And who were the early Templars, if not Godfrey de Bouillon and his knights and canons?

If any thing similar to this did happen it might help us to understand why the Templars were allowed to appoint their own priests. If Godfrey and his family (for example his brother Baldwin) searched for "treasure," perhaps this is what passed into the hands of the inner order of the Knights Templar.

I hope this short chapter illuminated some of the possibilities that Godfrey and his knights found something in the Holy Land that related to his family ancestry, and in particular, his Merovingian roots. In response to his successful find, Godfrey may then have wanted to form a "hermetic and alchemical" society, that indeed might have existed up to modern times. This group may indeed have been "guardians" of knowledge or treasure relating to Jesus, and the origins of Christianity. We must consider the fact that Godfrey and his family, once installed as rulers of Jerusalem (and with the help of their Templar creation) eventually had direct access to the three major areas of Jerusalem that were associated with hoards of treasure (the Temple Mount, Mount Sion itself, and the Holy Sepulcher).

The Ladies of the Grail

Salome: The Lady of the Grail
By Yuri Leitch

Although there has been much speculation as to the true identity and nature of Salome, based upon evidence I have uncovered, I believe that the lady Salome of Herod's household had some connection with the Holy Grail.

In past writings, I have made the observation that there was a Salome present at the Crucifixion of Jesus, when Joseph of Arimathea created the Grail. As such, I think it is important to look deeper into the possible role Salome played within this historical context.

The name Salome is mentioned in the Gospels at least three times. The first time that Salome is mentioned, she is described as dancing for her stepfather, Herod Antipas. In return for this, she requests, and is given, the head of John the Baptist on a platter. (In the story of Peredur, in the *Red Book of Hergest*, the Grail is described as a "head upon a platter.")

The second time that Salome is mentioned she is with Mary Magdalene, watching the crucifixion of Jesus (presumably witnessing the Roman Centurion as he pierces Jesus through his side with a spear; which is further "Grail procession" imagery).

The third time that she is mentioned, Salome is accompanying Mary Magdalene (carrying embalming spices) to Jesus' tomb in the garden of Gethsemane (thought to have been the garden of Joseph of Arimathea).

There never seems to have been a woman more intimately connected with the Holy Grail than Salome. So why haven't other grail researchers paid more attention to her before?

The answer to the previous question is, I believe, that every authority on the topic seems to have assumed that Salome of Herod's court, and Salome of the crucifixion, are actually two different women (and that Salome was a very popular name in biblical times). Personally, I find this a very strange distraction from the obvious.

So, how many women named Salome were there? I cannot find any evidence in the four gospels specifically stating that there were two women called Salome. Presuming that the Biblical authors would have differentiated between different people, it seems entirely plausible the varying Salome references all deal with the same person.

Still, if we consider the "two Salome theory," why not take it further and say that there were actually three women named Salome? (The bible doesn't specify that the Salome watching the crucifixion was also the same Salome that went to the tomb of Jesus. Maybe the Salome that went to the tomb was a third Salome? After all, it was a very popular name in biblical times!) No, I don't think so.

Rather, I think that all references to Salome refer to the same woman, otherwise the bible would separately distinguish them with a secondary name or a descriptive term (such as in the case of the two "Simons"—"Simon called Peter," and "Simon the Zealot"). For example, we might have mention of "Salome of Herod's House," and "Salome of the Crucifixion," and so on. However, the Bible does not do so. Therefore, I believe that there is only one Salome, and I have yet to see any evidence contrary to this. So why try to confuse the situation?

My first assumption as to why the established authorities should insist upon two separate women named Salome was a simple one. I assumed that the "two Salome theory" came about because it seemed to be absolute nonsense that the "bad" Salome, responsible for the death of John the Baptist, could also be the "good" Salome attending the crucifixion. But then, Salome was never truly "bad." It was not Salome who killed John the Baptist. She merely "danced" when her stepfather told her to, and requested John's head because her mother told her to. What was she to do? Say no to her parents, the rulers of Galilee?

Salome. Drawing by Yuri Leitch.

Herod had long wanted John the Baptist dead, but he feared the reprisals of the Judean people. Salome was nothing but his alibi and scapegoat.

The popular image of Salome as some sort of sexy erotic temptress, dancing the "dance of the seven veils," is a recent artistic invention (none of which is mentioned in the bible). The bible does not even specify how old she was. She is only described as Herod's stepdaughter. (The "dance of the seven veils" was brought to the public arena by the imaginative pen of Oscar Wilde, who, in his play "Salome," considered the theme of women's sexuality as potentially destructive of man's higher spirituality. Wilde has his heroine dance the seven veils, which was inspired by the Babylonian legend of the goddess Ishtar's descent into the underworld, passing through seven gateways.)

However, even if Salome was a "bad" person (and there is no evidence to say that she was), full of shame and guilt for her role in the death of John the Baptist, she could have repented. As a "sinner," she would have been perfect candidate to be part of Jesus' entourage, for as Jesus is quoted as saying: "It is not the healthy who need a doctor, but the sick. But go and learn what this means; 'I desire mercy, not sacrifice', for I have not come to call the righteous, but the Sinners" (Matthew 9:12).

I think that I have reasonably shown that there is no contradiction or difficulty in both Salomes (of the "Two Salome Theory") actually being the one and the same person. In fact, I find it very strange that the historical scholars have tried to insist otherwise.

Still, I realized that there must be another reason for the "Two Salome Theory," and the discovery that this led me to was startling, for even the bible itself attempts to play down her importance.

After dancing for Herod, Salome is next mentioned as having attended the Crucifixion. Only the Gospel of Mark mentions her by name, where as the other three Gospels are vague (and seem deliberately so). Talking about the Crucifixion, the Gospel of Mark states: "Some women were watching from a distance: Mary Magdalene, Mary the mother of James the Younger, and of Joses, and Salome. In Galilee (remember, Salome was a princess of Galilee), these women had followed him and cared for his needs" (Mark 15:40).

The Gospel of Matthew tells almost the same story: "Many women were there, watching from a distance. They had followed Jesus from Galilee to care for his needs. Among them were Mary Magdalene, Mary the mother of James and Joseph, and the mother of Zebedee's Sons" (Matthew 27:55).

For some reason, Matthew adds, "and the mother of Zebedee's Sons," and deliberately avoids saying the woman's name being referred to (which, when compared with the Gospel of Mark, is quite obviously, Salome).

So why does Matthew refuse to call a spade a spade? At least Matthew tells us something that we didn't already know about Salome: She was the mother of Zebedee's Sons, which means that she was the mother of James and John, the "fishermen" from Galilee (and two of Jesus' 12 disciples!). (Note: In Arthurian myth, the Grail is kept in the castle of the Fisher King.)

So although the Gospel of Mark told us that Salome was at the Crucifixion with Mary Magdalene, the Gospel of Matthew attempted to avoid mentioning her name. The Gospel of Luke is even worse! It mentions no women by name at all!

The Gospel of Luke says: "When all the people who had gathered to witness this sight, saw what took place, they beat their breasts and went away. But all those who knew him, including the women who had followed him from Galilee, stood at a distance, watching these things" (Luke 24:48).

The Gospel of Luke does not, however, consider it worthwhile to mention any of these women by name at all! Stranger still, though, is the final Gospel (that of John), that states: "Near the cross of Jesus stood his mother, his mother's sister, Mary the wife of Clopas, and Mary of Magdala" (John 19:25).

John's account is astounding! We have "Mary of Magdala," whom the other Gospel writers also mention. Additionally, we have "Mary the wife of Clopas" (who must be the same person as "Mary the mother of James and Joseph," as Salome has already been shown to be "the mother of Zebedee's Sons"), and we have "his mother's sister," who can only be equated with Salome!

So, not only is Salome the mother of two of Christ's 12 disciples, she is also his mother's sister—Jesus' Aunt! If this contention is true, it brings about two very profound conclusions.

First, at least two of the disciples were Christ's own cousins, rather than just "fishermen" picked up randomly from the seaside.

Second, Christ's own mother was thus a "daughter" of Herod! (This, of course, gives an entirely different slant on the story that Mary and Joseph had to flee to hide their child from the eyes of Herod!)

Herod was of the Herodian family. He was appointed to govern Galilee by Roman rule. To make this a smooth process, the Herodian kings married into the families of the Judean aristocracy, descendents of David and Solomon. King Herod, under the watchful eye of the Roman Empire, ruled over the Judean people of Galilee, and the Judeans hated him. At the time, John the Baptist was unifying the Judean people into religious zeal. Herod wanted John dead, but he likely feared that the Judean people would revolt if John was murdered.

Herodias, Salome's mother, was a blood relation of Jesus, his mother Mary, and others. The sympathies of both Herodias and Salome may have been with their Judean kin, but they may have been bound by Herod's court through political marriage. (There is no evidence to say that Herodias was happily married to Herod, the brother of her recently dead husband.)

After Salome had danced for Herod, he offered her "anything she wanted, up to half his kingdom." Salome asked her mother what she should request. It is possible Herodias told her to ask for John's head, knowing full well that it would start a civil war (an act that turned out to be the catalyst of Jesus' movement against the Sanhedrin of the Temple and against Rome.

It has also been said of the "Two Salome Theory," that the Salome of the Crucifixion was "Mary Salome," one of the "three Marys." (The "Three Marys" is an artistic icon of the Christian world. They are usually depicted at Jesus' tomb. At his birth there were three kings, and at his death three queens—it is artistic, esoteric symbolism, and fantasy.) There are actually four Marys mentioned in the Gospels: Mary the mother of Jesus, Mary the mother of James and Joseph, and wife of Clopas, Mary Magdalene, and Mary the sister of Martha and Lazarus.

I cannot find anywhere in the Gospels a place where Salome is called "Mary Salome."

So in summary, Salome was the custodian of the head of John the Baptist. Salome was also related to the holy family, and the mother of two of the 12 Disciples. Salome was Christ's aunt (very similar to the role to Joseph of Arimathea, who is thought to have been the Uncle of Jesus).

Additionally, Salome was said to have stood at Golgotha ("the place of the skull") with Mary Magdalene, and was witness to the martyrdom of her nephew, Jesus. She watched as he was pierced through his side by the "Spear of Destiny" (that profound Grail-related artifact). Salome and Magdalene then went to Christ's tomb, carrying embalming spices (during which time, Joseph of Arimathea was constructing the Holy Grail).

Finally, according to later tradition, the remnants of Christ's entourage left the Holy Land in a boat, and traveled to Europe to "spread the word." Along with the Virgin Mary, the Magdalene (whom settled somewhere in France), and Joseph of Arimathea (who then took the Grail to Britain), was "Mary Salome." Where she settled, no one knows.

The Legacy of Mary Magdalene
By Lynn Picknett

But Christ loved her more than all the disciples and used to kiss her often on the mouth. The rest of the disciples were offended by it and expressed disapproval. They said to him, "Why do you love her more than all of us?" The Savior answered and said to them, "Why do I not love you as I love her?

(From the Gospel of Philip, in *The Gnostic Gospels*)

The Resurrection.
Drawing by Yuri Leitch.

In 1989, when the first woman was ordained a bishop of the American Episcopal Church, it was not her spirituality, determination, or outstanding qualifications for the job that drew comment from *Time* magazine, but rather her red nail polish. All eyes were on Barbara Harris primarily as a woman, not as a priest undergoing a longed-for initiation into the role of bishop. Her red nails were seen as the blatant badge of the vamp—and surely such women have no place in God's house?

There were, and still are, many men who believe that any woman who presents herself at the altar as a priest before God must belong in that category. They see women as bringing the unholy "taint" of sexuality to the very presence of God—especially when menstruating—and reveal a primitive fear that goes back to the darkest and most ignorant of ages.

Mary Magdalene, the Church's eternally penitent reformed prostitute, is now the unofficial patron saint of women's ordination. And not for the first time in history, men see her as the symbol of a threat to their power—a clever and seductive woman who, even in her penitent contortions, somehow still threatens to usurp male prerogatives.

Bishop Harris was one of the trailblazers of women's ordination into roles of power in the United States (although women were only allowed to enter the first rank of priesthood in 1976, while the first American woman rabbi was ordained in 1972). It took longer for the rest of the world to catch up with this enlightenment: In September of 1992 the Anglican Church in South Africa voted in favor of allowing women into the priesthood. Two months later, by a mere two-vote margin, the Church of England finally agreed to allow females at the altar (although amid much ado and furor), with many vicars "going over" to Rome in their disgust at what they perceived to be a perversion of God's holy and inviolable law.

The evidence of undignified public squabbles, fighting, and distinctly non-Christian epithets that flew about the Synod's hallowed halls was to scar the Church of England to this present day, and has created cliques and cabals that seem to spend more time fighting each other than they ever do caring for their somewhat forlorn and neglected flock (many of whom fail to see what the fuss was about, and react with pleasure to having a motherly figure to turn to at their local vicarage).

As for the Catholic church, it has repeatedly reacted with strenuous denial that there is a case to answer. The Vatican's 1976 Declaration on the Question of Admitting Women to the Priesthood justifies excluding them on the grounds that women's bodies are different from that of Jesus, and it is therefore impossible to allow them to officiate as his representative at the altar before God.

More than 20 years later, little has changed. In Pope John Paul II's Apostolic letter (the Ordinatio Sacerdotalis of John Paul II, May 22, 1994), he stated: "…in order that all doubt may be removed regarding a matter of great importance, a matter which pertains to the Church's divine constitution itself, in virtue of my ministry of confirming the brethren (Luke 22:32) I declare that the Church has no authority whatsoever to confer priestly ordination on women and that this judgment is to be definitively held by all the Church's faithful."

Jesus—not to mention his own Apostle of the Apostles, Mary Magdalene—might have had something to say about this.

Although barely mentioned in the New Testament, Mary Magdalene has always been a major figure to groups of "heretics," such as the Cathars of southern France, and the Knights Templar. Many of the former were so convinced that she and Jesus were lovers (not, however, husband and wife) that they went willingly to their deaths at the hands of the Albigensian Crusade. The Templar's Absolution, on the other hand, was: "I pray God that he will pardon you your sins as he pardoned them to St. Mary Magdalene and the thief that was put upon the cross." (See Malcolm Barber's *The Trial of the Templars*.) There was also a saying of which the knights were fond: "…he that drinks deepest will see the Magdalene."

Yet, to the average churchgoer she is of mere passing interest—the prostitute from whom Jesus exorcised seven devils, a shadowy figure in the background, behind the more famous male disciples such as Simon Peter, who went on to create what became the Roman Catholic Church (for many years the *only* Christian Church in western Europe). Recently, there have been timid attempts—usually on the part of American feminists—to have the Magdalene acknowledged as the leader of the female disciples, or even the "13th apostle." Although this makes the more misogynist hackles rise within the Church—they refuse to accept that Jesus had any female disciples, despite the fact that they are listed as apparently appearing out of nowhere at the time of the crucifixion. (See, for example, Mark 15:40, where the disciples are described as having "followed" Jesus, which is the literal meaning of "disciple." Also, an interesting thought is that it seems the women provided for the men as they roamed about on their mission—but if the Magdalene was, or even "had been" a prostitute, this implies that Jesus had been living off immoral earnings!) A little delving reveals a totally different story, and one that the Church has assiduously covered up over the centuries. Although the canonical gospels are largely Magdalene-free, the same cannot be said for many of the texts rejected from the New Testament by the Council of Nicaea in the fourth century.

Indeed, it is interesting that most of the more coherent Gnostic books (some of which surfaced in Nag Hammadi in 1945) that have an equal claim to be considered as "authentic" (such as Matthew, Mark, Luke, and John) feature her so prominently that, aside from Jesus, Magdalene is the *star*. In the Gospel of Philip, the Gospel of the Egyptians, the Gospel of Thomas, and the Gospel of Mary (Magdalene), she is not only Christ's constant companion (the word used is *koinonos,* which specifically means "sexual consort"), but his inspiration—he calls her "the All," (an old title of the goddess Isis), his catechizer, and the focus of his life. It appears he was so besotted with her that "there was nothing he would not do for her…even raising Lazarus for her…."

The male disciples, however, found her hard work, and her very assertive part in the mission so unlike the passive background role expected of Judaean women that they may have implied she was a foreigner.

In a late-Gnostic book, *Pistis Sophia* (Faith-Wisdom), Mary goes to Jesus and complains that Peter had threatened her because "he hates me and all the race of women." It seems that as long as Jesus was around to protect her, she could avoid Peter's hate, but after the Crucifixion she had to flee to France, according to the legends.

What is particularly interesting is that the Gnostic books describe how the male disciples were completely demoralized at the crucifixion—especially Peter, who was drunk—but that Magdalene made a rousing speech and fired them up to begin their lives as apostles. The irony is that if she had left them lying in a sodden heap her own followers would have had a much better time of it, for the Church of Rome would never have been founded (leading, of course, to the systematic persecution of her followers—be they the Cathars, the inner circle of the Templars, or other groups). It is no coincidence that the Inquisition was established specifically to deal with the Cathars, and their remnants in the form of the so-called "witches" of the Languedoc, in southern France.

Magdalene's "church" (really a fluid, inspirational movement) was the opposite of Peter's organization. Whereas his was dogmatic to a fault, inflexible, and brutal to any who disagreed with the established doctrine (and hugely misogynist to this day), hers was intuitive and compassionate, and maintained a high regard for the feminine, and for the rights of women. The early Gnostics for whom she was the great inspiration had women preachers, prophets, and baptizers—even bishops, although this inconvenient fact has been explained away, or flatly denied, for centuries. The "heretics" believed passionately that Jesus had given the Magdalene the title "Apostle of the Apostles," that placed her squarely ahead of Peter and all the other disciples, both male and female—and implicitly made her Jesus' successor.

Indeed, the whole authority of the church lies in the doctrine of the Apostolic Succession, the idea that as Simon Peter was the first to see the risen Jesus he was obviously the "Chosen One." Yet, even a cursory reading of the New Testament reveals this to be complete nonsense. For example, in Mark 16:9, it is states that: "When Jesus rose early on the first day of the week he appeared first to Mary Magdalene...." The only possible theological argument against Mary having Christ's authority is that women could never be counted as disciples or apostles. Yet the heretics knew she was all that, and much, much more—so where is St. Peter's authority?

Significantly, the early church fathers knew about her importance and her relationship to Jesus, but deliberately chose to suppress it in a cynical campaign to rob women of their power and promote a celibate Jesus. What Jesus had wanted was of absolutely no consequence.

Thanks to the ultimate persuasion of fire and sword, the Church successfully created a new Magdalene, a frail, pathological penitent completely at odds with Mary the Magnificent, who (or so the "forbidden" gospels claim), Jesus used to kiss on the mouth in public, and whom he made the center of attention at all times. This craven image was the blunt instrument with which the Church sought to beat up any woman foolish or brave enough to have both a brain and a voice. This travesty of the wild and wonderful woman who preached and baptized, and put heart into the traumatized men, became the patron saint of female *shame*.

Through her new image it was made known in no uncertain terms that sex was sinful, and therefore children were born in sin and shame (and that what Jesus had done when he "converted" her was free her from a life of sexual depravity). Yet, even so, the Church's Magdalene is not the patron saint of joyful new beginnings, but a pallid, swooning thing, who masochistically weeps and wails, obsessed with the shame of her past—hardly grateful to Jesus, one might think.

Jesus himself would not recognize this female eunuch, but surely he would have accepted at once the Magdalene of the heretics, his partner in (at least) sacramental sex, his spiritual *equal*, and his chosen successor. Even suspending disbelief for a mere moment, the picture is so radically different from the one still trotted out from the pulpit on Sundays, that the reality of the age-old cover-up suddenly leaps into sharp focus.

Because of the church father's fear and hatred of the Magdalene, and everything she stood for, the whole of history was changed. For example, women (and many men, as well) were denied a voice in their communities, and even an education. The church ruled every aspect of life with the iron grip of fear. Children were abused, sexual love was demeaned, and as a result, generation after generation of dysfunctional, angry, and brutal leaders terrorized their own European countries, and those they claimed as their Empires.

Although it would be simplistic nonsense to claim that every instance of callous disregard for human rights grew out of the terror of the Magdalene's power, she was the ghost that eternally haunted the corridors of power, especially in the Vatican. And fortunately, she still does. Who knows? Soon she may emerge into full view. And *this* Mary Magdalene will be apologizing to no one for being a woman.

The Knights Templar and Lady Wisdom
By Damian Prestbury

The Knights Templar were warrior monks, and, as were many monks from this period of history, they were devotees of "Our Lady," or "Lady Wisdom" (the feminine counterpart of Christ).

If we read the Temple rule we see that the term "Our Lady" is used a large number of times (just as much, and perhaps even more so, than "Lord," "God," or "Jesus Christ"). In certain sections of the rule, the terms "God" and "Our Lady," or "God" and "Lady St. Mary" are mainly used, while the term "Virgin" is not used much at all. Also, the only saints named in full in the rule (outside of the references to feast and fast days), are St. Peter, St. Paul, and St. Mary Magdalene. Mary Magdalene even has the epitaph of "glorious," that suggests a certain emphasis upon her as a saint, as the other saints do not receive such an epitaph. In the section of the rule referred to as the "Reception In to the Order" is the following:

> ...but you should say the hours of Our Lady first, and those of the day afterwards, because we were established in honour of Our Lady; and so say those of Our Lady standing and sitting.
>
> ...And the hours of Our Lady should be said first, except the compline of Our Lady, which should always be said last in the house, because Our Lady is the beginning of our Order, and in her and in her honour, if it please God, will be the end of our lives and the end of our Order, whenever God wishes it to be.

In the section of the rule that deals with the ceremony of reception into the Order, the candidate is pledged to seven certain promises dedicated to the Order, and to personal conduct by promises to the Divine (as expressed with the epithet, "God and to Lady Saint Mary").

In the section dealing with the opening, conduct, and closing of chapters to do with awarding penances for brothers of the Order, according to their various transgressions, there is an interesting mention of Lady Wisdom towards the closing of the chapter:

> …on behalf of our father, the pope, and on behalf of you who have given me the authority, and I pray to God that He, through His mercy, and for love of His sweet mother, and for the merits of Him and of all the saints, forgives your sins just as He forgave the glorious St. Mary Magdalene.

I think it is important to consider the monastic side of the Templars. In order to do so, one first needs to look at the Cistercian/Benedictine teachings of St. Bernard of Clairvaux, who was the Templar's own patron and spiritual father. (It was this monastic saint and reformer who was responsible for giving the Templars their rule. Some Templars who were imprisoned at Chinon during their persecution for heresy composed a prayer mentioning how St. Bernard was the founder of their religion, which belonged to Our Lady—the quotes from the rule above confirm this.)

St. Bernard's teachings were primarily based upon the spiritual love song in the Old Testament, the "Song of Songs," attributed to King Solomon. The saint composed a large number of lectures based upon this scriptural text in which he identified the black Shulamite, the sacred Bride of the Bridegroom as the Church personified as the soul of souls, and each individual soul. The Bridegroom he identified was Christ. The love of the church-collective, soul-individual soul for Christ, and vice versa, was the love of the Bride and Bridegroom in this spiritual love song.

St. Bernard also had a special devotion to the Black Virgin, who had commonly been known to represent not only Mary, but also this black Shulamite of the Song of Songs. This Mary has also been associated with certain "Pagan" goddesses too. According to some researchers, many Black Virgin sites are situated near Templar sites.

The Song of Songs was not only considered sacred by St. Bernard and his Cistercian followers, and perhaps the Templars too, but was also held in similar high esteem by the famed Talmudic Rabbi, Rabbi Akiva, who was a contemporary of Christ. Akiva, a great cornerstone of Talmudic Judaism, as well as a great authority on the Kabalistic teachings of the book of Genesis, described the "Song of Songs" as the holiest of all scriptural text. Many other rabbis have also accepted this view. The teachings of the Kabalah have a unique focus on Lady Wisdom as the Shekinah, Yahweh's consort and bride, who was known to the Greeks as Sophia. Mary was considered by both the orthodox and the unorthodox as an incarnation of Sophia-Shekinah.

Another feature of the Black Virgin is that she appears in places that have harboured Kabalistic academies, such as the Languedoc, in the South of France. There were also Kabalistic academies in Troyes (where the Templars received their rule, and where the court of it's leading and founding members—also attended by Jews—was located). The Cistercian Mother house at Citeaux hired Jews to help the monks better understand the Hebrew of the Old Testament. The members of the council at Troyes, who gave the Templars their rule, consisted of the main bishops and abbots from the region of Burgundy (from which St. Bernard had come, and from which the southern cult of the Magdalene had been brought north and established).

Thus not only would Lady Wisdom have been recognized by the court of Troyes in the popular devotion to the Virgin, but the Magdalene as well. (The oldest church in Troyes is dedicated to Mary Magdalene.)

So, on the monastic side of the Templars, we have evidence of devotion to the sacred Eros of the cult of the Virgin Mary, the Black Mary, and St. Mary Magdalene. Additionally, there were also some Kabalistic teachings around during this period that focused on Shekinah-Sophia, bride of Yahweh.

Next, I would like to consider the military and knighthood side of the Templar order. From the early 12th century, when the Templar order was growing, so grew the focus of chivalry upon Lady Wisdom and her damsels, by claiming them as the source of inspiration for the good deeds of chivalric knights. Perhaps this focus upon Lady Wisdom stemmed from associations with the Magdalene cult (that was later embedded within, and taken control of by the cult of the Virgin)? Perhaps it was this kind of Lady Wisdom current that had entwined with the traditions of various oriental, occidental, and European Goddesses, and emerged entwined within chivalric circles in the Septimanian and Languedoc regions.

This growing emphasis upon Lady Wisdom and the damsel as the source of chivalric inspiration would most definitely have overlapped within the minds and hearts of Templar knights, because of the connections with chivalry as a whole. The "awakening" of the Lady was also reflected in the changes of attitudes towards women that were developing, both within the church, and within the secular feudal society of knights, nobles, kings, and servants. Thus the way of the troubadour emerged, finding voice in the expressions of song, poetry, story, and music.

This emergence of Lady Wisdom was an expression of the political and religious currents of thought with regard to the refinement of the "way of the knight" in general (which both the troubadours and the Templars expressed in their own ways).

Templars, as well as many other knights of the day, would have been quite aware of (and some, quite sympathetic with) the songs, poems, stories, and music of the troubadours. It was the knights and clerks in the courts of Languedoc who were the original troubadours—and their influence was felt by the knights and clerics in the courts of the north as well. Their original homeland, the Languedoc, was also the home of the Magdalene cult, which, along with the troubadour ideal, came north.

The compositions of the troubadours were based upon poetical technique, originality, and a desire to serve Lady Wisdom. The famed Lady was seen as generally unattainable, but that did not stop the troubadours from trying to attain her love, as well as a symbolic union with her. Through this service, the troubadours did gain poetical and knightly grace. And the sweetness of the lover's pursuit of the loved one attained, in their eyes, mystical and worldly heights. The troubadour revelled in this love as "separation," as opposed to love in union (that was deemed as an even "higher" union).

The Lady desired by the troubadour was half human, and half divine. He saw Lady Wisdom incarnate in the lady of this world whom he loved, the one to whom he wrote and dedicated his poems, the one whom he served with knightly acts and courtly etiquette, and the one that he sang his songs about. She was the primary source of the courtly and virtuous qualities he developed and aimed for.

To the troubadour, who was sometimes a knight, and sometimes a clerk, the setting for the amorous pastimes of servile love of Lady Wisdom and her earthly representative, was the feudal society of the Languedoc and the model of the court. Later, certain developments of the "troubadour way" in the north of France and Germany spurned writings that taught the amorous ways of divine and earthly love in settings other than the court and feudal society. In these writings, spiritual and material love danced her dance in the quaint, beautiful, and pastoral country life.

But these were not the only developments of the way of the Troubadour. These northern developments found their origin in the voices of the northern troubadours, and the minnesingers in Germany. (The minnesingers wore a badge, upon which was Our Lady of Halle—in present day Belgium she is a Black Virgin.)

The troubadour of the Languedoc embodied a particular "type" of love—that being the love of married woman. In times when marriage was based mainly upon political, feudal, and economic incentives, love was often forced into the background, and conversely appeared within extramarital, "adulterous" ways. It was a time when the nature of love was being observed, along with its sometimes-flagrant disregard towards the strict conventions of such dry marriage arrangements. Love was seen as superior to the marriage system of the church and the secular society of the day (which tended to unite man and women together in the bond of cold economic and political strategy, rather than love). But although the troubadours of the Languedoc emphasised and glorified "adulterous" and "illicit" true-love unions, some of the minnesingers emphasized and glorified the bliss and joy of love within a "true" marriage (that contested the sad reflection of conventional marriage).

The love of Lady Wisdom was also developed in the court of Marie of Champagne in Troyes. Her court was likely attended by the troubadours of the south, who were patronized by her mother, Queen Eleanor of Aquitaine. This court was fabled in the romances as one of the great "courts of love." And as previously mentioned, these courts were attended by the Jews (a number of whom may well have perhaps been Kabalists). Cistercians would also have been in attendance, along with their peculiar "Marian cult" of St. Bernard, that had strong associations with Black Virgins. And of course, I should not fail to mention the knights who would have been there, along with their clerical and secular supporters. Within this medley of hearts there would have been a strong devotion towards the Magdalene, evidenced throughout this region. (It was in this court that the first Grail romance, *Perceval*, by Chretien de Troyes, appeared in the public arena. This romance of mystical and magical chivalry was elaborated and woven around in certain various ways by a succession of later authors.)

The Grail romances are romances of chivalry. In them the ethics and way of chivalry is set within a mystical land of fable. Chivalry, and its various limbs, become an alchemical formula for the attainment of the Grail (which bears similarities to the alchemists' goal of the philosopher's stone). The Grail romancers took the "troubadour way," in a sense, by relating such otherworldly chivalry to the service of Lady Wisdom, who held the object gained by such otherworldly chivalry—the Holy Grail. But the Grail romance is a separate strand of the teachings of Lady Wisdom from the troubadour strands of wisdom. They are epic in fashion, and the Lady ethic is centralized within a new court, so to speak, and thus associated with religious and monastic knights (including the Templars), as well as with the court of King Arthur of Breton fable, set within the context of a specific Christian mystery.

The Knights Templar were directly associated with the Grail knights, who guarded the Grail in Wolfram Esenbach's *Parzifal*. Esenbach was the son of a great minnesinger, and he was also a member of that brotherly order of the Templars, the Teutonic Knights.

Esenbach's successor, Albrecht Von Scharfenburg, elaborates further in his romances on the Grail knights of the Temple. Not only does the brotherly order of the Teutonic Knights—in the person of one of it's members, Esenbach—weave in Templar mystery with the Grail (for he does leave many guessing and many questions unanswered), but the other brotherly order of the Templars, the Cistercians, weave their own Grail romances as well.

The knights of the Grail, as featured in the romances, sometimes wore the Templar habit of a red cross upon a white mantle. Esenbach and Von Scharfenburg certainly weave in alchemy with the Grail, side-by-side with the Templars. Interestingly, alchemical symbols have been found upon Templar buildings in the Languedoc region of France. Also, Templar graffiti found on one of the walls at Chateaux Dome (wherein certain Templars were imprisoned) showed themes of the Grail story, such as Joseph of Arimathea obtaining the blood of Christ at the crucifixion in a Grail. Similarly, the Grail theme of the healed and wounded land relates to the legendary curse or blight brought upon the land of St. Martin du Vesubie, France, due to the Templars that were beheaded in this area.

In addition, a Templar knight was said to have written the Grail legend *Perlevaus*. It is in the Grail romances that Lady Wisdom relates to the Christian mystery, as well as to monastic knights. The Templars have been connected to the Grail, and the Grail themes could not possibly fail to attract any knight (Especially a Templar knight—who may well have been the model upon which the Grail legend was weaved in the first place).

Thus there is evidence that monastic and military influences were quite likely to have had their place within the heart of a Templar knight. We have the monastic mysticism of the Black Virgin church embedded within the "Song of Songs," as understood by St. Bernard of Clairvaux and his famed Cistercian order, along with possible Jewish and Kabalistic influences as well. We have the cults of the Virgin and the Magdalene side-by-side, both of which quite likely embodied certain strands of Pagan influences. And side-by-side with these currents of Lady Wisdom, we have the refinement of chivalry by the church, as well as by the troubadours, and later developments in Christian and Grail romances.

At the least, these influences must been seen as an important backdrop in understanding the mentality of the monk/knights of the age, including most of the Knights Templar. All important orders would have contributed an influence upon the cultural and mystical backdrop of the age. Certainly those connected to the Templars did as the Cistercians, troubadours, and so on. And so, why not the Templars themselves?

Mary Magdalene: Mistress of the Grail
By Ani Williams

The Earth lifts its glass to the sun
And light—light is poured.
A bird comes and sits on a crystal rim
And from my forest cove I hear singing.
…An emerald bird rises from inside me
And now sits upon the Beloved's glass.
I have left that dark cave forever.
My body has blended with His.
I lay my wing as a bridge to you
So that you can join us singing.

(from "The Crystal Rim")

Wooden Black Madonna, Rosslyn Chapel. Photo by Ani Williams.

Like pearls from an ancient lover's gift, Magdalene sites and legends are spread across a vast expanse, from Ethiopia to Palestine, Egypt to France, and north into the highlands and isles of Scotland. Crumbling chapel ruins, great gothic cathedrals, caves, symbols carved in stone, and stories of her coming and going remain like fragments of an old necklace, waiting to be found.

Magdalene can currently be seen rising from a long sleep. As the story of Sleeping Beauty, Magdalene and her people have been "drugged" into unconsciousness for 2,000 years by an extraordinary effort to suppress the "other half of the story," *her* story. From the moment that Peter's church formed the "rock" and foundation of Christianity, she was written out of the accepted doctrine (except for references to her as sinner, a woman from whom seven devils were removed by Jesus, and the one who dried the sweat on his body with her long hair).

Peter's religious authority stemmed from the church's acceptance that he was the first disciple to see Jesus appear after the crucifixion. Yet, three of the gospels claim that Magdalene was the first to see him in the Garden. The sacred Grail pattern, that requires presence of the feminine, was severed at the core during the founding of the Church. Yet, the pieces are revealing themselves to any who choose to awaken.

The reemergence of the Magdalene

*Mary is rising…she is rising to her heights…Our Mary will
not be cast down and bound up…and neither will her
daughters. We will rise, Daughters. We…will…rise.*

(from *The Secret Life of Bees*)

One of many recent dramatic appearances from Mary Magdalene
was in *Jesus, Mary, and Da Vinci*, the ABC Primetime news show that had
people buzzing nationwide. The show examined the questions concerning the true relationship between Magdalene and Jesus (both as companions, and possible intimates). The program acknowledged her status as
"the Apostle of the Apostles," and did not portray the penitent prostitute
typecasting that has been her "scarlet letter" for 2,000 years.

The program also examined the symbolism in Leonardo da Vinci's
"The Last Supper," and his portrayal of Magdalene sitting on the right
side of Christ, their two body positions forming a "V," a feminine symbol, and a chalice. Here are two excerpts from the program:

> There's no factual basis for that longstanding tradition
> that Mary Magdalene was a prostitute, a woman of ill
> repute.…Mary Magdalene is one of the greatest saints in
> the history of the church.

> I think it's entirely plausible to think that Jesus may have
> been married. It was a normal practice for Jewish men. It
> would also be normal not to mention that he had a wife.

I was struck by my granddaughter's epiphany as she watched the program. She realized that if Jesus and Magdalene really did have children,
she might actually be carrying that same bloodline. That is quite a different

legacy than thinking we are "less than" other people, or even worse "sinners."

As stated in a *Time* magazine article: "From the beginning, her view has been ignored, unappreciated. Yet she remains. She cannot be silenced."

Other recent Magdalene appearances include a feature article on Mary Magdalene in the August 11, 2003, issue of *Time* magazine, Dan Brown's popular novel, *The Da Vinci Code*, and numerous other Magdalene books released recently—all indicating her potent matrix is weaving its way back into our psyches. Through film, literature, revealed documents, and a growing interest in her story, Magdalene is finally rising from the hidden caves of our unconscious.

The Holy Grail romances and medieval Madonnas

The 300 years between 1000 A.D. and 1300 A.D., were a period of radical breakthroughs, filled with fresh new idealism, a renaissance of spirituality, and the time of the Christian crusades. Passionate expressions of art, rising ideals of romance, and visions of individual freedom and women's equality spread across Christian Europe.

This time period witnessed the birth of the Grail romances, courtly love, the song and story ministry of the Troubadours, the formation of the Knights Templar (guardians of the Grail and Magdalene mysteries). Additionally the devout Order known as the Cathars (from the Greek "katharos," meaning pure) originated, and came to be associated as protectors of the Grail legacy and the sacred union of Jesus and Magdalene.

It is important to keep in mind Eleanor of Aquitaine. Her passionate support of the arts, romantic love, and women's freedom fueled significant change, as well as incurring for herself many "Magdalene" labels. She was the only woman to be Queen of two countries (through her marriages to King Louis VII, of France, and later to King Henry II, of England, with whom she gave birth to Richard the Lionhearted). Additionally, Eleanor personally traveled to Jerusalem during the second crusade, and had close dealings with the Cathars and Knights Templar. (It was Eleanor's daughter Marie de Troyes, who was instrumental in the completion of Chretien de Troyes' Grail Romance, *Le Conte du Graal* (1190 A.D.), the earliest-known grail story written).

Aquitaine, France was a hotspot for the troubadours of courtly love, and Eleanor and Marie created the controversial *Tractus de Amore et de Amoris Remedia (Treatise on Love and the Remedies of Love)*, which includes 31 codes of romantic conduct meant to educate her male subjects in the romantic requirements of the newly emancipated women.

During this same period, there was a sudden rise in interest in the schools of Hermetic and Egyptian secret alchemical knowledge. It was also during this era that several hundred Black Madonnas were placed in chapels and cathedrals (as far east as Russia, and north into Britain). Ean Begg, author of *The Cult of the Black Virgin*, states that many of these Black Virgins were brought from the near east by the Knights Templar.

Lynn Picknett, author of *Mary Magdalene*, and *The Templar Revelation*, thinks that Magdalene may have even come from Ethiopia, a dark-skinned, powerful, and wealthy queen. These dark-colored mother and child images are often associated with Isis and Magdalene cults (the dark Mother Goddess nourishing her children), and with the hidden mysteries of the sacred marriage (or Hieros Gammos) and the alchemy of high-sexual magic. Similar "Madonna" images can be seen in Egyptian temple scenes with Horus at the breast of his mother Isis.

Black Madonna with Child, Salisbury Cathedral. Photo by Ani Williams.

From 1100 A.D. to 1300 A.D., hundreds of Gothic Cathedrals were constructed, inspired by the mystical visions of St. Bernard of Clairvaux, and his close involvement with the crusaders and the formation of the Order of Knights Templar. (It was also St. Bernard who wrote the first Templar's Rule during their formation in Jerusalem in about 1118 A.D., and who played a key role in their official papal recognition at the council of Troyes in 1129 A.D.) Templar symbols are found carved in these Gothic edifices, and display a rare fusion of Pagan and Christian roots that allude to the alchemical sciences of sacred geometry, sound, astrology, genetics, and the technology of transformation.

These great Gothic cathedrals, such as the ones at Chartres, Notre Dame, Salisbury, St. Denis, and Cluny were dedicated to Notre Dame, *Our Lady*, thought to be Magdalene. Most were also home to the Black Madonnas. As Paul Broadhurst and Hamish Miller state in *Dance of the Dragon*: "The huge number of Gothic cathedrals that were erected, as graceful and sublime as if they were designed in heaven, have yet to be surpassed for their dignity and spiritual potency, almost a thousand years later."

The sacred architecture employed in these majestic structures reflected a new "alchemical light and specific acoustical properties," Broadhurst and Miller state, that was conductive to the constant rounds of perpetual choirs maintained by the monks. Interestingly, it is precisely at these millennium shifts, when perpetual chanting becomes a device of the collective creative intention. Sacred music and chant is always with us, but surges in its necessary popularity at these crucial turning points, as during the inception of Christianity in the first century A.D., at the beginning of the first millennium, and now, write our "script" for the next 1,000 years.

If we read between the historical lines, a pattern can be seen here, with an inner circle of key players stirring the pot of change. These courageous and inspired pioneers of the spirit were laying the foundation for a future second millennium renaissance. Now is the time for us to remember the true story of our tribal myth, a story that embraces the Holy Grail of union, love, and beauty—a story that calls us to become empowered, whole, and fully human.

Magdalene as Christ's initiatrix

As Margaret Starbird writes in *The Goddess in the Gospels*, "...the sacred union of Jesus and his Bride once formed the cornerstone of Christianity...the blueprint of the Sacred Marriage, that the later (church) builders rejected, causing a disastrous flaw in Christian doctrine that has warped Western civilization for nearly two millennia."

Let us look at the following significant transition or initiation points in the life of Jesus that indicate Mary Magdalene was not only present in this life, but was the one who performed his most important ancient rituals and rites of passage. (These rites would have been performed only by one initiated into the deeper mysteries, and one who would have commanded a key position in the unfolding drama):

- Magdalene anointed Jesus with her alabaster jar of spikenard prior to his being captured and crucified, and seemed to have knowledge of the overall plan before it was clear to the other disciples. The following excerpt from Solomon's "Song of Songs" (1:12), implies that Magdalene was following a much more ancient ritual tradition, in which the bridegroom, or king, is anointed by the bride or high priestess, and this rite most likely predates the passionate love poems of Solomon and Sheeba.

- The Magdalene was present (along with Jesus's mother (Mary), the disciple Salome, and John the Beloved), at the cross, while the other disciples were in hiding—too overcome with grief and fear to even appear! According to Magdalene and Templar historian and author Lynn Picknett, when Magdalene went back to find the male disciples and rally them out of their fear and total hopelessness after the crucifixion, she actually gave the church to Peter (although, as the companion of Jesus, the ministry should have reverted to her!).

- Magdalene and Mary the mother anointed Christ's body with specific unguents (thought to alchemically aid in Christ's after-death journey), and then wrapped his body with linen in preparation for burial—certainly tasks only to be entrusted to those closest to him.

- In three of the Gospels, Magdalene is the first one that Jesus appeared to following the crucifixion. Jesus then said to her,

"Noli mi tangere" ("do not cling to me"), and as Starbird comments, the Greek translation of "tangere," meaning "cling," implies a more intimate relationship between them, rather than the Latin "to touch."

● According to the *Pistis Sophia*, a Gnostic text in which Jesus makes a grand reappearance after the crucifixion and teaches the disciples deeper inner mysteries, it is Magdalene's presence that dominated this dialogue with Jesus, and both her questions and answers indicated an "Apostle who knew the All."

This is a woman who definitely did not play a minor or casual role either during, or after, the life of Jesus. Although the historical documentation that refers to Magdalene following the crucifixion is interwoven with the legend and myth, many scholars say that it is quite possible that she had been married to Jesus. Although, according to her devout heretical followers, the Cathars of Southern France, they were unmarried lovers.

It appears that Magdalene continued the ministry that embraced the original purpose of Christianity in the years following the crucifixion. There are records of her having preached her message on the steps of the Temple at Marseilles (dedicated to the Goddess Diana), and that she had a strong following in southern France. Legends of her escape from Palestine to Egypt and France, and a further journey to Great Britain included her bearing the children of Jesus, being the figurehead of the Magdalene-Isisian Mystery Schools, and her retreat into the deep caverns of France and the areas around Rennes le Chateau, Rennes les Bains, and even into Glastonbury, England.

Rosslyn's secret codes in stone

Mary Magdalene is said to be the patron saint of the Knights Templar, and numerous signs of her presence can be found in Scotland, including indications of her children, and a Celtic Magdalene bloodline! Additionally, the Rosslyn Chapel, near Edinburgh, plays an important role in Magdalene's Scottish legacy.

This mysterious chapel, often referred to as a "Bible in Stone," or the "Chapel of the Grail," and perhaps built with the Chapel Perilous in mind, mirrors the design of Jerusalem's Temple of Solomon. The building of Rosslyn was begun in 1446, and completed 40 years later by Sir William St. Clair, the third and last Prince of Orkney. (Members of the Sinclair family claim to be descendants of the Davidic, Merovingian bloodline, through the children of Jesus and Magdalene.)

The prolific symbolic carvings in Rosslyn, many of which relate to the Knights Templar, present a striking integration of both Christian and Pagan motifs. As Karen Ralls, former assistant curator of Rosslyn, comments in *The Templars and the Grail*:

> Templar, Masonic, Rosicrucian, and Christian symbolism...are woven throughout...In many ways, the carvings at Rosslyn Chapel are about the interplay of opposites and complements...light and dark, male and female, life and death.

According to Andrew Sinclair, member of the St. Clair/Sinclair clan, the name Rosslyn "...is said to derive from the old Scottish ROS-LIN or Rosy Stream, suggesting the blood of Christ."

One of the persistent legends regarding Rosslyn is that the Holy Grail is buried within the Apprentice Pillar inside the chapel—possibly the same grail or cup that contained Christ's blood, and is said to have been carried by Joseph of Arimathea from Jerusalem to Britain via France. Could this Grail, brought from the Holy Land by either Joseph of Arimathea, or the Templars, have finally ended up at Rosslyn?

Other sacred and precious items originally from Solomon's Temple and Medieval Europe, brought north for safe-keeping (out of reach of the hands of the Europe's "power brokers") are said to have been placed at Rosslyn. As Ralls states: "The Ark of the Covenant, the mummified head of Christ, the Holy Grail, lost scrolls from the Temple of Jerusalem, Templar Order treasures…a Black Madonna and more have been thought to lie within its vaults." (Some others say the Templars' Grail head is that of John the Baptist.) The Sinclair family history also speaks of the Holy Rood, a piece of the original crucifixion cross, being carried to Rosslyn and buried within its vaults.

Sacred sites and Nature's Temples

Many significant pilgrimage sites across the world are built upon the ruins of earlier temple structures, the locations chosen strategically for the natural earth-spirit currents already present. Common to spiritual centers such as Chartres, Glastonbury, Rosslyn, Iona, Glen Lyon, Sedona, and Mayan and Aztec pyramids, we find numerous crossing energy currents, or ley lines, underground water streams, caves, and places of great beauty and power. These have been places of pilgrimage for thousands of years. This is certainly the case with Roslin Glen, with its winding river Esk, many caves, and rare varieties of flora. When walking through the glen, one senses that this is a place of both sanctity and magic, and it is this sense of the sacred that provided original inspiration to build temples, stone circles, and altars at these locations.

Rosslyn Chapel's carvings read similar to a dictionary of numerous varieties of flora, including mysterious representations of aloe (or agave) and maize. The prolific images of plant and flower varieties found in many Templar-related sites reflect some varieties of flora unknown in the north, but native to the Middle East and beyond. The Sinclair clan claim that their ancestor, Prince Henry Sinclair, sailed to America in the last decade of the 1300s, about 100 years before Columbus (whose ships flew the Templar banner with the flayed red cross), and founded Templar sites in Nova Scotia, Rhode Island, and Virginia.

Magdalene and the Mary Chapels

Barry Dunford, author of *Holy Land of Scotland*, spoke of the Mary Chapels and alignments through the heart of Scotland. He said there is a straight line connecting Montrose (mount rose) on the eastern coast,

Grail Knight, St Mary's Church, Grandtully. (Wooden ceiling mural c. 1636 A.D., commissioned by the Stewart family.) Photo by Ani Williams.

through the St. Mary Churches at Grandtully and Fortingall, to the western Isle of Iona. Another alignment runs east from Marywell, through Fortingall, and on to Tobermory (the "Well of Mary"), close to another key Mary Chapel at Dervaig, on the Isle of Mull. These lines indicate an ancient pilgrim's path, full of "birthing Mary" images and legends.

For example, St. Mary's Church at Grandtully has a wooden ceiling mural (c. 1636 A.D.) depicting numerous Templar and Grail images. Included are two pregnant, female "angels," a Grail knight, a unicorn and lion, and the Judgement Tarot card (including skulls and the black and white checkered floor, similar to the Templar beauseant banner).

Interestingly, this unusual medieval painting at St. Mary's Church, Grandtully was commissioned by Sir William Stewart, and the Royal House of Stewart claim to carry the Holy Davidic Grail Bloodline (both these lineages claim the unicorn as their symbol).

Following on the ancient pilgrim's path toward the Isle of Iona, one must cross the Isle of Mull, a naturalist's paradise. In Kilmore ("Kil" = church, "More" = Mary) Church at Dervaig, Mull, there is an intriguing stained glass window image, which could be Jesus with a pregnant Magdalene! The stained glass window was made circa 1905, when the

Judgment, St Mary's Church, Grandtully. (Wooden ceiling mural c. 1636 A.D., commissioned by the Stewart family.) Photo by Ani Williams.

present church was built, although a much older Druid site was there before, as the adjacent stone circle indicates.

Dunford pointed out that if, as the local Christians believe, the window depicts Mother Mary and Joseph, then Mother Mary would have the halo and Joseph would not. In this image however, the male figure has the halo, and this would indicate that it is Jesus (and obviously not with his pregnant mother), holding hands with a pregnant Magdalene.

A striking connection here is that the commissioning of this window appears to be by a Thomas Eversfield, named on a church plaque, and displaying two Templar crosses. Was Eversfield a member of the Knights Templar, and privy to secret information regarding the Holy Grail Bloodline?

Just across the sound from Mull, lies the Isle of Iona, once called Innis nan Dhruidhanean (the Isle of the Druids), where several legends speak of Magdalene giving birth to a child, and living her last days in a cave on the island. A crumbling ruin of an old Mary Chapel sits behind the great Abbey, where the presence of Magdalene is still palpable.

Just behind the Abbey is a hill called Dun-I, where legend says St. Bride sang love songs daily, calling to her lost bridegroom. According to Fionna Macleod, author of *Iona*, two old prophecies say that Christ shall come again upon Iona, and when "she" returns it will be as the "bride of Christ, and the daughter of God."

As Christian mystics and pilgrims traveled the paths between these spiritual sites, they would ultimately journey southwest to Rosslyn and Edinburgh. During my meeting with Robert Brydon at Temple Village near Rosslyn, he mentioned an important early chapel in Edinburgh dedicated to Magdalene, known throughout the western kingdoms as a fertility site, where women would send items to be blessed for healthy, successful births.

I reflected again on my granddaughter's liberating epiphany while watching the *Jesus, Mary and Da Vinci* film, regarding the genetic inheritance of Holy Blood, and what this Scottish presence of Magdalene and birth associations could mean for a Celtic Grail Bloodline!

The rose of Rosslyn

"…I flame above the beauty of the fields; I shine in the waters; In the sun, the moon and the stars, I burn."

—Hildegard of Bingen

The rose, with its anagram of "Eros," has long been associated with "Our Lady," whether in relation to her role as Mary the Mother, as Magdalene the Lover, or as Saint. It has also been associated with the heart of Christ, the Rose of Sharon. The five-petaled rose, Rosa Rugosa, is the earth's oldest known variety of rose, and is a repeating symbol present at many Templar church sites.

The unusual solid stone barrel-shaped ceiling of Rosslyn Chapel is divided into five sections, and is covered with carved five-pointed stars, lilies, roses, and other flowers. These stars have an ancient association with Venus, Isis, and Magdalene, and are also found on the ceilings of Egyptian temples. (The pentagram's proportions are a perfect example of the Golden Mean, or PHI ratio, and the sacred geometry used in ancient temple architecture). Another section of the ceiling containing a series of cubes is said to correspond to PHI and a Fibonacci musical scale.

Dunford says that Roslin (the original spelling) refers to the Rose Line, a possible old earth meridian, and a well-used pilgrim's route running through Rosslyn. (The Rose Line runs southward on the early mystic's pilgrimage path to Avalon, and ultimately to Santiago de Compostella, in Spain. In fact, the clamshells—received as confirmation that one had truly completed the long road to Compostella—are still left as offerings on an altar stone within Rosslyn's Lady Chapel.)

At the front of Rosslyn Chapel stand three famous pillars (the Master Mason's pillar, the Journeyman's pillar, and the Apprentice pillar—these are said to represent Wisdom, Strength, and Beauty). At the top of the Mason's pillar are carved angelic musicians. At the base of the Apprentice pillar are eight dragons, from whose mouths come vines, which spiral up and around the pillar (said to represent the Scandinavian myth of the eight dragons that lie at the base of Yggdrasil, the Ash Tree that binds together heaven, earth, and hell). Legend states that the gifted apprentice, who carved the extraordinary detail of the Apprentice pillar, was murdered by his jealous master. We find a similar story and great intrigue, regarding the demise of Hiram Abif, the Master Mason of Solomon's Temple in Jerusalem. What Hermetic secrets were these ancient masons protecting?

Rosslyn Chapel's only complete inscription appears on the lintel connecting the top of the Apprentice pillar to the south wall, and is carved in Latin upon a spiralling ribbon of stone. The English translation follows (as quoted in Robert Brydon's 2003 Rosslyn Chapel Trust booklet, *Rosslyn and the Western Mystery Tradition*):

> Forte est vinu mo fortior est rex fortiores sunt muliers
> sup (er) om (nia) vincit veritas).
> Wine is strong; the king is stronger; women are stronger,
> but above all the truth conquers.

According to Brydon, this inscription is connected with the Royal Arch Degree, and refers to the words and wisdom of Zerubbabel, of the lineage of the Royal House of David. In the year 536 B.C., the people of Judah were released from their captivity in Persia, and under the leadership of

Prince Zerubbabel, they all returned to Jerusalem, and began the building of a new temple upon the ruins of the old Temple of Solomon. Is this fantastic inscription on the arch next to the Apprentice pillar telling of a Scottish or Sinclair connection with the Davidic-Grail bloodline? Is it reminding us that without embracing the feminine, that truth is out of reach?

From the Master Mason's pillar radiate four arches, and four more extend from the Apprentice Pillar, each with 64 cubes (perhaps alluding to the 64 genetic chromosomes). Along with the DNA spiral symbolism on the Apprentice Pillar, this theme is mirrored "coincidentally" in Rosslyn's nearby genetic farm, where the world's first cloned sheep and chickens were created! Is all this an uncanny allusion to genetics of a grail bloodline or the alchemical secrets of life contained in the blood and guarded by the Knights Templar, Guardians of Magdalene's legacy?

Indications are that it is quite possible that Magdalene and Jesus did have children. Magdalene and/or her children could have come as far north as Britain after the crucifixion, and if they did, there could be a Northern Celtic Holy Bloodline, in addition to the southern France bloodline, which spread a Christ/Mary genetic inheritance throughout the Western world.

I do believe Magdalene is calling us to reclaim the sovereignty and emancipation of the human soul, at the beginning of the second millennium and a crucial turning point for Earth. Now is the time to rewrite our global myth. The planetary alignment and lunar eclipse of November 8, 2003, with its six-pointed Star of David pattern is a powerful symbol for this re-integration of male-female, the alchemy of the union of opposites. Magdalene's return signals a fusion of dimensions of consciousness fragmented for 2,000 years, giving birth now to a potent healing force and opening the Grail of the Heart.

The Templar and Related Mysteries

The Franks Casket, Sabine Baring-Gould, and the Sangreal
By Yuri Leitch

The Reverend Sabine Baring-Gould, a prolific 19th century author, wrote more than 150 books, including the well-known hymn, *Onward Christian Soldiers*. In his most famous work, *Curious Myths of the Middle Ages*, he records and recounts the legend of the Sangreal.

According to the legend of the Sangreal, Joseph of Arimathea was present at the crucifixion of Jesus Christ. When Jesus was pierced in his side by the spear of the Roman Centurion, his blood and bodily fluids gushed forth, and Joseph collected the holy blood into the cup of the last supper—and this cup, sanctified by the blood of Christ, became the Holy Grail, or Sangreal.

Apparently, this act of devotion upon Joseph's part, angered the Jewish authorities so much that they threw Joseph into prison, and left him there to die of thirst and starvation.

Approximately 42 years later, when the army of the Roman Empire (lead by Titus) sacked Jerusalem, Joseph of Arimathea was found to still be alive! Joseph was then set free. The power of the Sangreal, secretly kept in his possession, had kept him alive for over four decades! Titus, witnessing this miracle, then received baptism from Joseph. Soon afterwards, Joseph set sail for Britain, taking the Sangreal with him. When Joseph of Arimathea finally died, he passed the Sangreal on to his nephew.

In the centuries that followed, King Arthur and his knights would consider the search for this sacred cup the most important of all their missions. It is this theme that inspired all of the earliest Arthurian romances of the 12th century, and it is from these romances that almost all Grail evidence originates.

This has led some authorities to damn the Grail stories as being nothing but 12th century inventions, and that the Sangreal legend of Joseph of Arimathea is nothing but a fabrication. Sabine Baring-Gould was aware of these accusations questioning the authenticity of the Sangreal story. (His own telling of the story is comprised from two 12th century sources: *Perceval*, by Chretien de Troyes, and *Parcival*, by Wolfram Von Eshenbach.)

In defence of the Sangreal legend, Baring-Gould states that Chretien and Von Eshenbach could not possibly be the inventors of the Grail story, as there exists in the *Red Book* (a volume of traditional Welsh legends) a tale that he claims is indisputably the original version. According to his claim, the original was a Druidic-Pagan mystery, that was adapted to Christianity by a British hermit around 750 A.D., (and predates the 12th century romances by more than 300 years.

The "Red Book" that Baring-Gould referred to is the *Llyfr Coch Hergest*, which is better known as *The Red Book of Hergest*. It is a compilation of

traditional Welsh romances that embody the Arthurian theme and characters. However, it is impossible to say whether its contents pre-date the
12th century writings of Chretien and Von Eshenbach, as the "Red Book"
was compiled at the end of the 14th century. Therefore, you cannot tell
for sure, just how ancient (or recent) the stories of the "Red Book" may
actually be (it is even possible that Chretien and Von Eshenbach actually
predate the contents of the *Red Book of Hergest*).

How Baring-Gould arrived at his date of around 750 A.D. I don't
know. However, Baring-Gould may have been in the know, because there
is evidence that clearly shows a knowledge of the Sangreal story did pre-
date the Arthurian Romances of the 12th century.

There is, in the British Museum, a small whalebone box that depicts
Titus and the Roman army, sacking the Temple of Jerusalem, and a small
person huddled in the corner of the Temple, holding a cup-like object.
This eighth century artifact is called the "Franks Casket," and it predates
the writings of Chretien de Troyes and Wolfram Von Eshenbach by
almost 400 years!

The Franks Casket, contrary to its name, has absolutely nothing to
do with the Frankish culture, or its people. It actually takes its name from
the kind gentleman who presented it to the British Museum, Sir Augustus
Franks.

The Franks Casket is approximately 13 centimeters high, 23 centi-
meter long, and 19 centimeters wide. It is ornately carved from whalebone. It is covered in Anglo-Saxon rune scripts. Every external side of
this box intricately depicts scenes of Biblical and Saxon/Nordic themes.
Its runic inscriptions are written in both old Northumbrian Anglo-Saxon
and Latin (the script on one side is actually an encoded script—without
vowels—that scholars are still trying to interpret).

There are so many enigmas about this box that it deserves in-depth research of its own. But what is of particular interest in this case are the front and back sides of the box.

The back of the Franks Casket depicts the sacking of the Temple of Jerusalem by the Romans, and in the corner of the temple is a small character offering the Romans a cup-like object. The runic inscription reads, "Here fight Titus and the Jews. Here the inhabitants flee from Jerusalem." A separate word reads "Judgement," and another "Hostage."

The front of the casket is even more enigmatic. Unlike the other sides of this box, the front is divided into two illustrations, and the runic inscriptions that surround the imagery say absolutely nothing about the scenes it encompasses. The inscription reads: "The fish beat up the Seas on to the mountainous cliff; the King of Terror became sad when he swam on to the shingle" and then a single word, "Hronasbon" (which means "Whalebone"). The whole inscription is merely a riddle to tell you what the casket was carved from.

Yet, the front illustrations are very important. On the right-hand side is the nativity of Jesus, depicting the Three Wise Men acknowledging the newborn Jesus as the King of Judea. Above their heads is small rune-script spelling the word "Magi." On the left-hand side is a scene from Norse tradition depicting the famous elfin smith, Wayland, working in his smithy with customers present.

At first glance, these two scenes seem out of context, and the runic inscriptions that surround them give us little explanation. But this box is well-conceived. Nothing on it has been carved due to artistic whim and fancy. So what connections are there between Wayland the Smith and the nativity of Jesus?

Wayland the Smith is an elfin smith. He is neither a man nor a god, but a stellar entity. To the Saxons he was immortalized as the Dog-star Sirius. His job was to make magical weapons and sacred artifacts for the Norse gods and goddesses. The Magi are giving Jesus gifts of Kingship—gold, frankincense, and myrrh.

But there is much more to it than this. At Wayland's feet is a crumpled body of a decapitated man. In one hand Wayland holds the decapitated man's head in a large pair of Blacksmiths tongs. And perhaps most interestingly of all, in Wayland's other hand he holds a cup-like object identical to the one held by the small figure in the Temple of Jerusalem (seen on the back of the Franks Casket)! Furthermore, scholars have suggested that Wayland is actually making a ritual drinking vessel from the skull of the decapitated man's head.

Now, it is a Christian-world bias to think of elves as little men lurking around the bottom of the garden. To a Saxon, an elf was an intermediary between men and the gods. Many famous elves were immortalized as personifications of the constellations. On the lid of the Franks Casket is a scene depicting Aegil the Archer, who is none other than Wayland's own brother (who is symbolized by the constellation Orion). Elves, to a Hebrew mind, would be considered angels, and prior to Christianity Saxons would have considered angels to be elves (they were all "shining ones," who help mankind).

So, to morph up mythologies, on the front of the Franks Casket we have the nativity of Jesus, and Wayland the "angel" making a magical drinking vessel from a human skull. On the back of the casket we have a figure being set free from the Temple of Jerusalem, holding the same magical vessel. There is already a lot of food for thought here, and the Franks Casket has many other secrets I am sure.

In *Perceval*, by Chretien de Troyes, the grail is considered to be the cup in which Joseph of Arimathea collected the blood of Christ. In the story of Peredur, in the *Red Book of Hergest*, the Grail is not a cup, but rather a decapitated head upon a platter. And if Sabine Baring-Gould is correct, the Peredur story is from the same era as the Franks Casket. (Incidentally, the place where Jesus was crucified was called "Golgotha," meaning "the place of the skull." The biblical lady Salome asked for someone's head upon a platter.)

The Knights Templar were said to have been the guardians of the Grail. They were also accused of worshipping a "head." Maybe both assumptions were true. Perhaps the Grail is both a cup and head (a ritual drinking vessel made from a human skull, and maybe even one made by angelic/elfin forces).

In the four gospels of the New Testament there is only one decapitation mentioned, and that is the beheading of John the Baptist (who is known to have been especially important to the Knights Templar). Maybe it was John's skull that was made into a ritual drinking vessel, a vessel that was magically enchanted to be an oracle of wisdom. And maybe upon Golgotha, the place of the skull, Joseph of Arimathea collected in this vessel the blood of the Judean-king bloodline as it poured out of the side of Christ. That would be one very heavily charged magical artifact!

Perhaps most tantalizing of all is the following connection: It is the lady Salome, of Herod's household, who was responsible for calling for the head of John the Baptist. In the gospel of Mark, as Jesus is dying upon the cross, his death is witnessed by the women in his life (his mother (Mary), Mary Magdalene, and most inexplicable of all, Salome). Then, Joseph of Arimathea requests that Pilate provide him with the lifeless body of Jesus.

Separated from each other by only a couple of sentences, and sharing the same final scene in the death of Christ are Salome (the custodian of John the Baptist's head), and Joseph of Arimathea, the original custodian of the Grail.

The Larmenius Charter and the Legitimacy of Modern-Day Knights Templar
By Vincent Zubras

Contrary to what "mainstream historians" declare (they are only quoting what the old Roman Church of the Crusade period wants everyone to believe), the Knight Templar Order *did not* meet their demise after the seven-year-long persecution by the Church that ended with Jacques DeMolay being burnt at the stake. This was simply what we of the Modern Era call the end of the "First Phase" of the Order. (This was the crusade-period Order, that lasted from its inception in 1118 (though some believe it was actually more likely 1114), to the death of DeMolay in 1314.

As DeMolay was approaching death, he likely knew that once he recanted his confession to the Inquisition he was doomed. So, he verbally "transmitted" the Grand Mastership of the Order (through remaining underground Brethren of the Order in Paris) to his "number-two man," that being the Palestinian-born Christian and Knight Templar, Seneschal, Johannes Marcus Larmenius. Larmenius, at the time, was fairly aged himself, and was holding the last of the remaining Templar Order together on Cyprus. Following the death of DeMolay, Larmenius held the Grand Mastership of the Order until 1324. At this point, he had a document drafted entitled the "Charter of Transmission" (historically referred to as "The Charter of Larmenius").

In this document, Larmenius states that he has grown too old to continue the rigors of the Office of Grand Master of the Order, and further "transmits" his Grand Mastership (with the approval of the General Council of the Order), to the next ranking Templar in line, Franciscus Theobaldus.

Larmenius Charter. From the private collection of Vincent Zubras.

Theobaldus, at that time, was the Prior of the Order at the Priory of Alexandria in Egypt. Theobaldus accepted the assignment, and signed the document. From that point, up until 1804, each Grand Master or controlling General Council Secretariat Official has signed the document. The Charter was written in a well-known Knight Templar "Codice" (coded writing) of the time—an alphabet based on positioning of the portions of the Templar (Maltese quad-triangled) cross. When decoded and translated, the charter has proven to be 13th and 14th Century Latin. Still, some naysayer historians claim the document is a hoax.

(This document is also referred to as the "Charta Transmissionis," or the "Charter of Transmission," as its sole function was to "transmit" the Grand Mastership of the Order under the then-dire circumstances (and thus safely maintain the integrity of the continuation of the Order itself), and to legitimize the historical, lineal descendents of the Knight Templar Order into the future.)

The charter is the written verification giving credence to the belief that the greater portion of the Order had "gone into hiding" in France, and around the rest of the world, after being "secularized" by the Papal Bull *Vox in Excelso* of 1312, issued by Clement V (the puppet Pope of the evil French King, Phillippe IV, or "Phillip the Fair"). The Order came into semi-public view in Versailles, France in 1705, when a Convent General of the Order elected Philippe (then Duke of Orleans, and later Regent of France), to the Grand Mastership of the Order. However, there is no *known* reference to the existence of the Larmenius Charter from those proceedings. However, there would normally be no "public mention" of the document anyway.

The document's existence was later publicly revealed around 1803 by the then-Grand Master, Bernard Raymond Fabre-Palaprat, a French doctor close to the court of Napoleon. Palaprat also revealed the history of the document as well. Since then, the Order flourished predominantly in France.

In the mid 1800s, the Grand Mastership went to Britain, and later to Belgium. In this latter case, the Grand Master was not elected, but rather the office was held "in regency" by the Council General and Grand Secretariat of the Order (located at that time in Brussels).

It is a historical fact that the German Army, under Adolf Hitler, invaded Belgium in World War II. Hitler was well known to be a practitioner of the occult (or "black") arts. One of the first things he did after the invasion was send the gestapo (secret police) to Brussels to seek out the Offices of the General Secretariat of the Order of the Temple. This occurred in 1942. Hitler believed he might find, through the records of the Order, the secret location where the Templars had hidden the Ark of the Covenant. (It was believed by various historians that the Templars had excavated under the Temple of Solomon, while quartered there during the crusades, and found the ark, and other treasures, and secreted them out of Palestine and back to Europe.)

An interesting point: If you study further, you'll find that the story line behind the movie *Indiana Jones and the Raiders of the Lost Ark* was largely based on actual history. Hitler believed the ark had magical powers, as claimed in the Bible, and that possessing it could help him rule the world.

It is a bit of the Order's historical lore that, on the night before the Gestapo showed up, then-General Secretary and Regent and Guardian of the Order, Emile Clement Vandenburg, gathered up all the records of the Order and secreted them out of Belgium, across France, across the Pyrenees Mountains, across Galicia (Northwestern Spain), and into the neutral area of Portugal. He presented the records he had, and conferred the Regency of the Order to the then-Marshall (equivalent to a Grand Prior) of Portugal, a Portuguese nobleman, Don Antonio Campello Pinto Pereira de Sousa Fontes.

Fontes kept the Regency and Guardianship of the Order throughout World War Two (he was never elected the Grand Master), and continued to hold such after the war was over.

Some historians have claimed that Vandenburg supposedly demanded the return of the records and the Regency to Belgium after the War. Fontes (again, supposedly) refused, stating that Vandenburg had *confirmed* to him upon its transfer that the transmission of the Regency and Guardianship was complete and permanent.

As the story goes, the old Belgian group was going to try to file a civil court case in Portugal, or try "by whatever means," to get Fontes to return the records and give up the Regency and Guardianship. However, right at that point, Vandenburg was killed in a car accident in Belgium, and no one ever pushed the issue on Fontes after that.

Fontes continued to build the Order around the world until the time of his death in February of 1960. Then, something else unusual happened. It was revealed that Fontes had willed the Regency and Guardianship of the Order to his son, 30-year-old Don Fernando Campello Pinto Pereira de Sousa Fontes (apparently this was considered a "willable holding" under Portuguese law). Fontes' son assumed the Regency and Guardianship of the Order at that point, and took leadership of the Order.

This is another point our "historical naysayers" have complained about. Not only did Fontes refuse to return the records of the Grand Secretariat to Belgium, but now, after his death, the Convent General (the general membership at large) of the Order was supposed to convene and elect a new Regent (or take the further step to elect a Grand Master—according to its statutes, and as stated in the old Templar Rule of the ancient Order).

However, these naysayers, as I call them, were wrong. Fontes' Regency and the Guardianship of the Order were confirmed by a subsequent Convent General.

Still another element of contention is that Fontes introduced an amendment to the statutes that set up the following factor: If a Grand Master was not elected by the Convent General within six months after the close of the *previous* Convent General, the Regent of the Order would automatically assume the Office of Grand Master, and the Regent would hold, effectively, the combined Offices of Prince Regent and Grand Master. When the six months passed, the office was passed to Dom Fernando. It is my understanding that the next Convent General meeting confirmed Don Fernando to this position of combined offices (and he remains the Grand Master and Prince Regent of the Order to this day).

Some of the dissidents of the Order in Spain split off from the legitimate Order (under Fontes' rule) sometime in the 1970s or early 1980s. Under the leadership of another Fernando, the Spaniard Fernando Toro y Garland, they set up their own Order—stealing the same title of the International Order, the coat of arms, the Cross, and so on, and "subtitled" their Order the "International Federated Alliance." This group of dissidents is generally referred to as the "IFA group."

Another schismatic coup by dissidents in the United States, Britain, Germany, and parts of a few other European countries, occurred in 1995. A group of "military egotists" broke away and attempted to steal the Order. This was a coordinated effort by some senior former military members and a number of "civilians," who were also members of the Order (this included British, German, Scottish, and most of the Grand Priory in the United States). The American group separated themselves further through a trumped-up Federal Court Civil Lawsuit claiming "trademarks violations" against another group formed directly by Grand Master Fontes in the United States.

This turned out to be the largest split to date within the Order. Since then, these schismatic groups have gone off and formed their own organizations, again stealing the Order's title, Cross, and so on, and claimed their own supposedly-elected "Grand Masterships."

The important part of this whole story is that Grand Master Dom Fernando Fontes is still internationally recognized as the true Grand Master, and carries with him the legitimate lineage of the Larmenius Charter. He currently directs the Order from the Offices of the Grand Magistery in Porto, Portugal. When he passes away, the remaining true and legitimate Convent General will come together and elect a new Grand Master. (Fontes is now 70 years old, still in good health, and is in the process of rebuilding the Order after the harm the schismatics have caused.)

Loyalists in North America (those few who retained their Templar memberships with the Grand Master in Portugal) took back the old, original name of the ancient Order of Knights Templar (the Order of Poor Fellow-Soldiers of Christ and the Temple of Solomon, post-titled "The Knights Templar"), and used the formal Latin title (Ordo Pauperum Commilitum Christi et Templi Solomonis, Equites Templi, or OPCCTS) in the United States, Canada, Mexico, and the Carribbean. OPCCTS is in confirmed and permanent "fraternal relations" with the Order in Portugal. OPCCTS recognizes the "legitimacy and supremacy" of Fontes as Grand Master (although by virtue of the Order's structure, and the limitations of the U.S. Court Order, Fontes cannot hold direct control or authority over the Order in the United States). By desire and design, OPCCTS is very much an integral part of the International "Loyalist family."

OPCCTS strongly believes in the maintenance of the ancient historical norms of "the Old Order," and is structured very similar to the original Order in Templar Rites and Practices. It is a legitimate Ecclesiastical Chivalric Order of Knighthood, complete with a Fons Honorum, (a spiritual "Fount of Honors") according to Chivalric Law.

Abbot Henry de Blois, the Templars, and the Holy Grail
By Oddvar Olsen

Henry de Blois was the nephew of King Henry I (the devoted brother of Stephen of Champagne, and later King of England from 1135 to 1159). Prince Henry was the maternal grandson of William the Conqueror, and son of the latter's daughter (Adela) by Count Stephen of Blois.

Henry's father died in the Crusade at Razes when he was only 2 years old. Little is known about Henry's childhood. However, some sources have claimed he was nicknamed "the sage" (because he seemed to know and remember everything), and that he spent some years in the great monastery of Cluny, in Burgundy.

At the age of 23, Henry was appointed Prior of Monacute in Somerset, where his uncle, Henry Beauclerc, was planning to create a fine royal abbey. By this time, Henry de Blois had completed his studies in the seven liberal arts—trivium (grammar, rhetoric, and logic), quadrivium (geometry, arithmetic, music, and astronomy), and architecture as well.

In 1126, at the age of 29, Henry was appointed Abbot of Glastonbury. What he found there was an Abbey in a state of collapse, and monks who lacked even the bare necessities of life. Abbot Henry took immediate action, proving himself an excellent administrator and architect.

Keen on centralized administration and economic strength, he recovered and restored the monastery and manors at Mells, Uffculme, Camerton, Damerham, and the villages of Siston, Ashcott, Pedwell, and Moorlinch. He also built castles at Farnham, Downton, and Taunton, and supervised building at Merton, Wolvesey, and Waltham.

At Glastonbury alone he built a bell tower, chapter house, cloister, lavatory, refectory, dormitory, a beautiful building called the "Castellum," an attractive outer gate of dressed stone, a brewery, and stables for many horses. Additionally, he extended St. Dunstan's library.

By 1143, Glastonbury Abbey was described in the Doomsday book as "the wealthiest in England." It had taken Henry only 17 years to transform Glastonbury Abbey to a landmark in England. The Abbey was also becoming a center for pilgrimage and learning throughout the rest of the known world.

Only three years after Henry was designated the abbacy at Glastonbury, he became Bishop of Winchester. Here, at this splendid cathedral, he allocated parts of the south transept as a storage space for the cathedral's priceless possessions. Henry also designed the east end around the relics of St. Swithun, including the Holy Hole, where pilgrims could crawl underneath the relics to get closer to the curative powers (thought to emanate from the saint's relics). The illuminated Winchester Bible was also produced under the patronage of Bishop Henry (still unfinished at his death).

One of the finest buildings Henry had built was the Hospital of St. Cross, on the outskirts of Winchester. Some years later, Henry was to assign the guardianship of this place to the Knights Templar. The Hospital of St. Cross is Britain's oldest existing charitable foundation. It was built between 1133 and 1136, and dedicated to "13 poor men, so feeble and so reduced in strength that they can scarcely, or not at all support themselves without other aid." For the wandering pilgrims of today it is a heartwarming place to rest one's weary legs and receive their Wayfarer's Dole (a drink of beer and some bread offered in the Porter's Lodge).

Curious Stone Carving, St. Cross. Photo by Oddvar Olsen.

Incidentally, King Stephen (Henry's brother) and Queen Matilda were two of the greatest benefactors to the Templars. They gave the Templars land in London, Lincoln, and what was to be the largest Templar estate in England, at Cressing and Witham (which measured 1,400 acres).

Where the Templars located their Manors and preceptories was of major importance for numerous reasons. Many were built on ancient holy sites, along hills, or near holy wells. But the Templars also chose their locations for practical reasons. For example, St. Cross was one days' travel on horseback to their final night's sleep in England (at Holy Rod in Southampton), where early the next morning ships would be waiting to set sail for the crusades and the Holy Land.

The Templar's connection was growing stronger, and Henry supplied them with Purbeck marble for their main seat in England (Temple Church, in London). Henry was the first person in England to use Purbeck marble. This was a very difficult material to work with, due to its hardness. (He might have acquired the skills to work with Purbeck from his trips to Rome, most likely bringing Roman stonemasons back with him.) We do know about Henry's affections for aestheticisms—this is demonstrated in the *Narratio de Mirabilibus Urbis Romae* of Magister Gregory, where descriptions of Henry's purchases of great statues, both classical and Pagan, can be found. Unfortunately none, as far as we know, remain.

Henry was a patron of great writers, one being the Archdeacon, Gerald of Wales, crusader and writer of at least 17 books, and another the renowned William of Malmsbury. In William of Malmsbury's work, *De Antiquitate Glasttonie Ecclesie*, which he dedicated to Henry, he tells us that "the monk he knew personally, and in fact whom he served was shy, learned, and a great writer." Personally, Henry gave approximately 60 books to the great library at Glastonbury. He had books copied, such as Pliny's Natural History, the book of Enoch, and several other books of Origen, St. Jerome, and St. Augustine. The standard works of Bede, Alchane, and Addlehelm were included alongside medical treatises, the lives of the saints, and the basic primers of Greek and Latin grammar and rhetoric. In addition to these major works, a curious selection of older books, now lost or dispersed, were listed, which John of Glaston later described as the "Vetustissimi." The Vetustissimi were the books of the ancient ones, all copied before the Norman Conquest, especially under the great and active leadership of St. Dunstan. Henry also studied the book of St. Dunstan. The book deals with St. Dunstan's sorceries and divinations resisting the Devil, his alchemical formulae, and a mysterious Gnostic book called *Organum*, or *Primum Organum*.

Another thing that might be worth mentioning is the fact that the Welsh Mabinogion, which some scholars ascribe to had been written around 1060, were translated to English in the early days of Henry's tenure. The stories in the Mabinogion are apparently the first written sources mentioning King Arthur. Much was later written about King Arthur, his deeds, his knights, his round table, and the search for the Holy Grail.

One of the first grail romances is titled *The High History of the Holy Graal*. A curious book, its language and its profound explanations led the reader through a labyrinth of arcane legends. The author describes the local terrain around Glastonbury in so detailed a fashion that he must have been a local to the area—a person steeped in folklore and esoteric wisdom. This being the case, it is possible Henry de Blois may have written this monumental Grail Romance.

While drawing a 20th century illustration for *The High History of the Holy Graal*, Katharine Maltwood rediscovered, as John Dee had also stated, that there was a zodiac located at Glastonbury. (Maltwood had been asked to draw a map of the itinerary of the Arthurian Grail Quest around Avalon.) This great geomantic circle of giant effigies, 10 miles across and 30 miles around, delineated by hills and contours, and outlined in part by streams, depicted the zodiac. The 12 signs of the zodiac have been completed by man through the ages, by roads, paths and canals, and embellished by tumuli, ramparts, and lynches at nodal points.

Maltwood went as far as to claim that the zodiac was constructed by the Sumerians when they arrived in Britain thousands of years ago, and that the Knights Templar worked on it during their time of dwelling at Glastonbury.

If we look closer into Henry's family and relations, we will see the Grail connection getting even stronger. His cousin Theobald was married to Eleanor of Aquitaine's daughter, Marie (Chretien de Troyes being under direct commission by them). As Henry de Blois was also Chretien de Troyes patron, we have to take into consideration that Henry might have known about the Grail legends, and may even have been one of these early authors. (In the elucidation appended to *Comte Del Graal*, by Chretien, the authorship of one of the first grail books is ascribed to one famous fabulator named master Blishis—possibly a rustic intonation of Blois.)

The Latin version of the *The High History of the Holy Graal* is credited to a monk at Glastonbury. Cretien was very close to Eleanor of Aquitaine and her daughters, and he admittedly said that he had been given a grail book by them to be romanticized and read aloud at court.

If we proceed in the creation of the Grail legends, we find further intrigue. Eleanor married King Henry II. The story related from this time period is that during a visit to Wales, King Henry was told by a sage the exact place to start digging at Glastonbury Abbey. When the land between two pyramids was excavated in 1191 the remains of King Arthur and Queen Guinevere were discovered. So what we have here are a few people, very closely related, who served as the promulgators of the Grail story.

Henry's family can be traced as far back as Theobald the Cheath, the man who conquered Chartres in the eighth century. Chartres was a cult center of the Holy Mother, and one of 200 or so Black Madonna sanctuaries in France (most of them dating back to the 11th and 12th centuries). This might imply a continuation of an ancient veneration of the sacred feminine. (This came alive again with the Trouvers and Troubadours in the beginning of the 12th century, their enchanting prose and poetry of courtly love and chivalry serving as a vessel for a secret tradition for the initiated.)

The Grail legend is one of the most recognised of all stories from this time period, and Cretien seemed to held a major place of importance in those days. (We have mentioned one of the first grail romances by Chretien de Troyes, and the council of Troyes as being the place the Templars were given their "rule" by St. Bernard. Henry de Blois was a local to this area.)

In the 11th century Jews were hunted down and killed all over Europe, but there were a few places they found refuge, one of them being Troyes. The Counts of Troyes actually favored them, and beginning around 1070 several schools of Kabbalah were established. Along with Rabbi Rashi's commentaries on the Bible and the Talmud, two books in particular flourished there, *Seper Yetzirah* and *Bahir*. The *Seper Yetzirah* was allegedly written by Abraham, as dictated by God, for mankind to have a guide as to how the universe was created. I think we can see similarities in the Kabbalah, the Tarot deck, and the symbolism used throughout the architecture of the Gothic cathedrals.

Still, one must ask if the Grail legends portray any "secrets" at all? Though this may be a hard question to answer distinctly, what we must take seriously is the oral tradition of narrative folklore and esoteric symbolism. Stories of great heroes and poems were, to the esoteric, mediums to preserve and pass on knowledge from the master to the initiate. Not only this, the legends forged a paradigm to understand an imperceptible land, encoded in its universal symbolism.

William of Malmsbury detected hints of a mighty secret in the geometrical pattern in the church's mosaic at Glastonbury Abbey. Architect and excavator Frederick Bligh Bond, during his excavations in the early 19th century, also hinted there was to be found an astrological "wheel of initiation" pattern engraved there. Could this be an earlier version of the Round Table? Was this an initiation rite of the Knights Templar perhaps the itinerary of the Grail search?

Henry de Blois Tomb, Winchester Cathedral. Photo by Oddvar Olsen.

As Henry de Blois was appointed the See of Winchester, it is not really surprising that it is there we can find the Round Table, completed some 70 years after Henry's death in 1171. The table is a magnificent piece of 13th century workmanship. It is made of oak, is 18 feet across and nearly 3 inches thick, and weighs more than a ton. It is now on view at The Great Hall of Winchester. (The first literary mentioning of the Round Table was in Robert Wace's *Roman de Brute* (1155), which claims King Arthur seated his knights around the table so they could all be equal.)

When excavating the tomb of Henry de Blois at Winchester, they found a small ivory head, accompanied by a chalice. What we have here are two of the sacred objects that figure strongly in the Grail legends and Templar myths: the chalice, or Holy Grail, and the "head" rumored to have been worshipped by the Templars. Keith Laidler, in *The Head of God*, suggests that not only was John the Baptist decapitated, but Jesus as well, and that the Templars were in possession of their decapitated heads.

Elisabeth Jenkins, in *Mystery of King Arthur*, also adds to the questions surrounding the Grail. As she states: "One of the additions made by another hand to Chretien's *Perceval*, or *Le Conte Del Graal*, a prologue called the Elucidation. It speaks of "Master Blihis (Henry de Blois) as one…who knew all the stories of the Graal." Recently I have come across references that support the theory that it was Henry de Blois who first started looking for King Arthur's grave, and not Abbot Robert of Winchester, as some other sources claim.

There is a plaque in the British Museum depicting Henry de Blois presenting a gift to God. On the left-hand side of the plaque an angel holds a bowl (perhaps a chalice, or might it be the Holy Grail?). The bowl is opaque red with yellow, which adds a bright accent in the upper area of the plaque. The inscription on the plaque reads: "The donor might follow the offering to heaven; but not immediately, lest England weep, for war and peace, turmoil or tranquillity, depend on him."

Afterword—August 3, 2005

This is pretty much as the article appeared in the August 2002 issue of *The Temple*. I have spent much time since searching for further information on this luminous personality. As it happens, most commentators on antiquity, Grail legends, and the Templars seem to have completely ignored Henry de Blois. Why, I don't know. Personally, I think it is evident that he had a much bigger role in grail/history than has ever been acknowledged.

Without continuing the debate in greater detail in this work, there are a couple of things that has been brought to my attention that I would like to add.

The first deals with the quote from Elisabeth Jenkins' *The Mysteries of King Arthur* about Blihis being the person "who knew all the histories of the Graal." Jenkins actually thinks that this was a Welshman called Bleheries (who lived from 1100 to 1150), and that Giraldus Camrensis refers to Blihis as Bleheries as well. (At the time of writing the article, I was only provided with half the quote—having now read the text in full I felt it necessary to clarify.)

There is also some uncertainty as to whether it was Henry de Blois' remains that were found inside the Purbeck marble tomb in Winchester Cathedral. Nicholas Riall states, in his studies published by Hampshire Papers, that the grave may be that of William Rufus. Only a couple of weeks ago I came across something that may support this. In an old guidebook to Glastonbury Abbey it says: "Leland who saw the tomb says, 'At the head of Arthur's tomb, lay Henricus, Abbas (Henry de Blois) and a crucifix: at the feet a figure of Arthur; a cross on the tomb; and two lions at the head, and two at the feet.'" When this was deleted, or why, from the modern guidebooks, I have not yet been able to establish. However if this guidebook can be trusted, Henry de Blois' intimacy to Arthurian legends is at least established. Perhaps he even was the "fabulator famosus" who authored the early Grail romance upon which Chretien based his *Le Comte Del Graal*!

The Head on the Platter
By Yuri Leitch

As the mysteries surrounding the Holy Grail have perplexed many researchers throughout the years, I think it is important to consider not what a grail *is*, but what it *is not*. By doing so, some light might be shed upon other related areas, such as the legacy of Salome and the artifact known as the Franks Casket.

The two most common misconceptions I've encountered in my research of the Holy Grail are that a) it is a cup, and b) that it is a metaphor for a divine bloodline. I believe that both of these notions are wrong, and that pursuing them will only lead future researchers in a circular path that goes nowhere toward discovering the true grail history.

In the earliest literature, the Grail is called a "Graal," and it is described as the "holy vessel" from the Last Supper. For example, the opening lines of *The High History of the Holy Grail* read: "Here ye the history of the most holy vessel that is called Graal."

The Beheaded. Drawing by Yuri Leitch.

Later medieval Romancers assumed that the "holy vessel" of the Last Supper was the cup that Jesus used when he passed around the wine saying, "This is my blood." But the cup Jesus shared was not the only "holy vessel" at the Last Supper. As recorded in the Gospels, there was also present at the table another "Graal," somewhat different from the previously mentioned. To understand this more clearly, one must consider the linguistics at work in the situation.

"Graal" is a French word (the language in which the early romances were written) and refers to a large, deep platter. A graal is more properly known as a "geraldi," or a "geraldis." (In 13th century France, it was also referred to as a "graalz," or "graal.") A graal was a popular type of communal eating bowl, from which a small party of people could eat at the same time. As if attending a buffet, those attending a meal could tear off pieces of meat and dip bread into the gravy contained in the bowl. This type of vessel is described in the Bible, and to the 13th century French it would have been recognized as a "graal." For example, in Matthew (26:23): "Jesus replied, 'The one who has dipped his hand into the bowl with me will betray me.'"

So, the holy vessel of the Last Supper, the "Graal," was never intended to be understood as being a cup. This perception may have developed from the rigid fanaticism of Roman Catholic medieval Europe, and from the importance within the Catholic world of the Eucharist ritual (the drinking of "the blood of Jesus"). This idea, in turn, was continued by the later romance writers, who also described a "cup" in their writings.

Now, many people feel this notion of the Holy Grail as a cup is a widely accepted religious, occult, and spiritual symbol. And in my opinion, this error has hindered many investigations as to the true nature of the Grail.

The other popular misconception is that the Grail, under the name of "Sangreal," should be interpreted as "sang real" (or "blood royal"), and that it therefore represents the heritage of a divine bloodline.

This interpretation has been promoted by the secret order of the Prieure de Sion, as explained in book *The Holy Blood, Holy Grail*. (Originally, the word "grail" was changed in various writings to such forms as "greel" and "greal." Later, it became the "Holy Greal," or more accurately, the "Sancta Greal." Later still, this was shortened to "san greal" and "sangreal." The Prieure de Sion then split the word, creating "sang real." This is quite clearly a departure from the original meaning of the word "grail.") However, the authors of this book never state that "sangreal" means "blood royal," they only provide the information for their readers to consider. Nonetheless, in the 20 years that have passed since the book was published, this interpretation has come to stand as "Grail" dogma to many people, even though it is a complete corruption of the original meaning of the word. Bloodlines do have their role to play in the history of the Grail. For example, Sir Galahad achieves the Holy Grail because he is the son of Sir Lancelot, and both knights are descendents of Joseph of Arimathea's "Fisher King" bloodline, and as such, are destined to be guardians of the grail. But the meaning of the word does not change.

From this information I can draw several conclusions. First, the Franks Casket refers to the HolyGrail tradition, and depicts a head and a vessel. Secondly, the ancient Welsh romance *Peredur* (considered by Sabine Baring-Gould to date from the eighth century, though other scholars place it as late as the 10th century) speaks of a head "swimming in blood." And lastly, *The High History of the Holy Grail* speaks of a "holy vessel" (the "grail" of the Last Supper), which seems to refer to a deep serving platter. The Holy Grail, then, is not Jesus' cup of blood, but was rather the platter that held the Baptists decapitated head.

On November 30, 2002, I attended the first Templar Conference hosted by *Pharo.com*, at Templar Lodge near Edinburgh, Scotland. During dinner the evening before the conference, I had the opportunity to chat with author and researcher Lynn Picknett regarding John the Baptist (one of her favorite subjects). I talked to Picknett about the theory that the original Holy Grail was a "head on a platter," rather that a "cup," and asked her opinion regarding the theory put forth by Keith Laidler in *The Head of God*. (Laidler points out that in the Gospel of Mark, just prior to the description of King Herod's arrival to present Salome with the head of John the Baptist, Herod is described as being upset about the growing popularity of Jesus. Herod also considers whether Jesus is the reincarnation of John the Baptist.)

I fail to see the reasoning behind this, as it was supposedly John who baptized Jesus. Thus, if they were contemporaries, Jesus could not possibly be John reincarnated. Still, that is what Herod is described as considering.

(In an attempt to explain the "reincarnation," Laidler concludes that perhaps John had been dead for some time prior to Salome's request for his head, and that his head was one of Herod's prized relics.)

Picknett offered an alternative to this consideration. She suggested that perhaps it wasn't "reincarnation" as we know it, and that "reincarnation" is a mistranslation of the original text form the Gospel of Mark. It is possible, Picknett said, that the text should be translated to read that Herod feared Jesus was in possession of John's "spirit."

If Picknett is correct, the simplified story in the Gospel of Mark could read as follows: Upon hearing of the preaching and miracles performed by Jesus, Herod believed that Jesus possessed the spirit of John the Baptist. (The Gospel of Mark then goes on to account how Salome had been given the Baptist's head. It is not said what she did with it, but as a Jesus sympathizer—she was his Aunt, and in attendance at the Crucifixion—she may have given it to Jesus.) Perhaps Herod was worried that Jesus had been given "the head on the platter." We have already seen how there was a "sacred vessel" at the Last Supper that was later used by Joseph of Arimathea to collect the blood and sweat of Jesus.

If we suppose that Jesus and John were rival prophets and magicians, it would shed light on the accusations directed at the Knights Templar during their trials. We know that Templars were devoted to John the Baptist. We also know that they were accused of spitting on the cross. As they were rumored to be the guardians of the grail, we can see how they would have been accused of worshipping a "head."

The "Graal" is also mentioned in the Gospel of John, and if Jesus and his disciples really were enemies of the Baptist (and thought that, by possessing John's head, Jesus would be able to conjuring miracles—as Herod feared), the account of the Last Supper in the Gospel of John, is not only awesome, but also a little scary:

> Jesus answered, "It is the one to whom I will give this piece of bread when I have dipped it in the dish." Then, dipping the piece of bread, he gave it to Judas Iscariot, son of Simon. As soon as Judas took the bread, Satan entered into him.
>
> (John 13:26)

This may seem like a wild speculation. But if, on the behalf of Jesus, Salome had John the Baptist beheaded, then the spirit of John the Baptist could have achieved his revenge by taking possession of Judas Iscariot at the Last Supper (and thus bringing about the Crucifixion of Jesus).

Abraxas: The Seal of the Inner Order Templars?
By Oddvar Olsen

The Abraxas, used as a seal by the Knights Templar, has caused some misunderstanding within the scholarly community. To uncover the mysterious symbolism expressed by this seal, it is important to consider the historical origins of the artifact.

Most descriptions of the Abraxas allude to a figure "with a rooster's head, human torso, and with snakes as legs." Abraxas is also known as an a magical spell, a word used by Gnostics to personify deity, and the source of 365 emanations. This word also makes up the number of days in a year, when calculated by the Greek letters, as follows: A = 1, B = 2, R = 100, X = 60, S = 200. When added together, these total 365. (The word "mithra" adds up to 365 in a similar fashion. Both words have been venerated as Gods and symbols of totality.)

The Abraxas has been found on Hellenistic magic papyri, and on ancient and medieval amulets. Perhaps of kabbalistic origin, it is said to derive from Hebrew abra' kesa—"hide the four" (meaning God, and alluding to the Tetragrammaton).

The Swiss psychiatrist and psychoanalyst Carl Gustav Jung (1875–1961) alluded to the Abraxas in his writings:

> (Abraxas) is truly the terrible one…the sun and also the eternally gaping abyss of emptiness…magnificent even as the lion at the very moment when he strikes his prey down. His beauty is like the beauty of a spring morn….He is the monster of the underworld….He is the bright light of day and the deepest night of madness….He is the mightiest manifest being, and in him creation becomes frightened of itself.
>
> (Abraxas) is…a thousand-armed ployp, coiled knot of winged serpents…the hermaphrodite of the earliest beginning…the lord of toads and frogs, which lived in the beginning…the lord of toads and frogs, which lived in the water…abundance that seeketh union with emptiness.

> Abraxas is the god whom it is difficult to know. His
> power is the very greatest, because man does not perceive
> it. Man sees the summum bonuum (supreme good) of
> the sun, and also the infinum malum (endless evil) of the
> devil, but Abraxas he does not see, for he is indefinable
> life itself, which is the mother of good and evil alike.

The Abraxas' dualism is clear, so it is no surprise to us that the Abraxas symbolism was used by the Templars and the Gnostics. Its rooster's head represents "dawn" symbolizing the sun and the light, the human torso represents the earthly elements, and the cross and two serpent feet represents the darker elements. In its hands the Abraxas holds a shield (wisdom) and a whip (authority). So the Abraxas can be understood as the god that is half good, half evil.

The Templar's flag, the Beauseant (half white, half black—sometimes including a "cross pattee" in the middle) reflects the same symbolism. The Templars often acted as envoys between the Pope, kings, and other nobles, and served as negotiators. Being the "middlemen," they could quite easily have chosen to adopt certain parts of "heretical" knowledge and practises, thereby representing a cauldron of knowledge.

It is hard to find any evidence for the origin of the Abraxas. Some credit it to Persia, others to Egypt. The first written account that I have found states that the Abraxas was used by the Basillideans, a Gnostic sect from the second century A.D. The Basillideans were founded by Basillides of Alexandria, who was a disciple of Meander (who had been a pupil of Simon Magus). The Basillidean system had three grades—as did the Templars—the material, intellectual, and spiritual.

The doctrines of the Basillideans also have many points of resemblance to those of the Ophites. The patristic Origen suggested that the

Ophite sect of the early Christians forced its members to curse Jesus (according to Hammer, as quoted in Peter Partner's *The Murdered Magicians*), and accepted the Templars as successors of the Gnostic Ophites. The beliefs of the Ophites were similar to Jewish Kabbalism, with a succession of Aeons, Emanations, and Sephiroth, over which an Archon, or the angelic prince, presided. Their teaching was based on the belief that Simon of Cyrene took the place of Jesus at the Crucifixion.

Here in England, a respected author and researcher came across a man in Lichfield a few years ago who had found a Templar seal with the Abraxas figure on it. It had been discovered in a field with a metal detector. But when the researcher asked to investigate it, the discoverer of the seal refused and sent it to the British Museum (where, hopefully, it will see the light of day again soon).

Abraxas seal. From private collection of Oddvar Olsen.

An Abraxas seal from a temple in Paris (now housed in the collection of the French National Archives) bears the Abraxas figure with the inscription "Secretum Templi." This has led to the supposition that it was used by a secret, inner order within the Templars.

However, as the French researcher Michel Lamy points out in his 1997 book *Les Templiers, Ces Grands Seigneurs aux Blancs Manteaux* (*The Templars, the Great Lords of the White Mantles*) this seal was used on many mundane documents.

There is, for example, a document dating from 1214 that is signed and sealed by the Templar Preceptor of France, and deals with the division of a certain forest between the Order and the King of France. As Lamy comments: "One cannot say that this is a particularly hermetic text." (Lamy goes on to suggest that the term "secret" refers to the Abraxas being a seal that was used on particularly important documents. He points out that 10 percent of all Templar seals found had Gnostic origins.)

So, why did the Templars use the Abraxas seal? Did the Order only use it as Lamy had suggested? Or was it the seal of a secret Inner Order of the Templars? What is the likelihood that the Templars had a secret inner Order?

To claim anything for certain would be very brave with the scant evidence we possess. Still, the idea is very attractive, especially with the discovery of several manuscripts during the last few hundred years. For example: Fabre Palaprat declared that he had picked up a manuscript called the *Levitikon* (written in Greek), from a used book store in Paris in the early 1800s. The *Levitikon* presents Jesus as an initiate of the higher mysteries, and as having been trained in Egypt. Through its Johannite lineage, the *Levitikon* tells us that James (Jesus' brother) had continued the church ministry. The church continued with successive ministers until it was passed on to Hugh de Payen, the so-called first Grand Master of the Templars.

In 1877 a German Masonic specialist named Merzdorf claimed to have found, among other Masonic manuscripts, two Latin "Rules" of the Templars (purported to date from the 13th Century). One was the Rule for the "chosen brothers," and the other for the "consoled brothers." The first Rule describes the church as the "Synagogue of Anti-Christ," and stipulates an elect reception ceremony (involving various ritual kisses—one on the male member—and including readings from opening verses of the Koran). The latter Rule implies strongly that the Templars shared the doctrines of the Cathars, including that of the "consolamentumm," or mystical baptism. Still authenticity of these has yet to be determined.

I do not think we yet have enough evidence to say that the Templars had a "secret inner order." However, I have recently been referred to a text called *The Book of the Baptism of Fire* (the credence of this text needs to be ascertained, so I will just briefly mention it here). The text was apparently transcribed by the Grand Master in England (Robert Sandford), in 1240 A.D. It lists the different articles of *The Order of the Weather*. Some of the articles refer to both the "chosen" and "consoled" brothers. There is also mention of Baphomet and "the Secret Science of the great philosophy: Abrax and the Talisman." As there have been so many forged documents trying to establish and divulge "an elect secret Order and its mysteries," its authenticity will have to be proved before we can accept this as a historical document.

However, there are many indications that the Templars had an "Elite" guiding them. There are too many uncertainties about the legendary origin of the Order (and their first nine years while dwelling at Al-Aqsa Mosque), what they did and what they allegedly found, and the astronomical expansion of the Order in the following years. All of this speculation, of course, leaves open the possibility that the Templars had a plan as to what they were doing and where they were going.

The accusations against the Order include their holding heretical beliefs and secret meetings at night. Still, when looking at the existing recordings concerning the trials, they do not really prove anything (as they were written by the king's men—the accusers, who were not exactly neutral in their recordings).

When concerned with Abraxas as the seal of a secret "inner order," I think we will have to rely on Lamy's explanation. At least until more historical evidence comes to light.

Knights Templar House, Kelvedon, Essex
By Terence Wilson

In 1971, my wife and I moved to Kelvedon, Essex, England, where we purchased an old brick-faced terraced house on High Street. As the building was more than 400 years old, we came to discover numerous pieces of evidence as to it prior inhabitants. (One obvious indication hung on the front door of the house—a carved plaque reading: "Knight Templars Terrace 1861.") How-ever, we were assured that because the house dated from circa 1490, the name over the door was the only link with the Templars.

The interior of the building needed sub-stantial renovation, and much of our spare time was spent reno-vating generations of neglect. While work-ing in the large up-

Templar house, Kelvedon, Essex.
Photo by Oddvar Olsen.

stairs bedroom, I removed a layer of thin, rotten boards that were nailed to a substantial oak subfloor. It transpired that this subfloor was actu-ally nailed to the oak ceiling of the room below, and was comprised of huge carved beams roughly 23 centimeters apart, and which subse-quently branched out from an even larger carved beam that ran down the center of the room.

While cleaning these timbers I discovered, in a large crack in one of the beams, what appeared to be a fossilised dead rat encased in hard clay. On closer examination, I could make out writing. The "rat" turned out to be a tightly rolled piece of parchment, adding further to the mystery of the house (and its link with the Knights Templar).

When the parchment was steamed open, it revealed a page from a book (approximately 160 millimeters x 230 millimeters). Each side of the sheet was beautifully hand-written in 12th century Latin script, as follows:

> Pug...frib; Fr venit irib° orclunb° Et ut cognouert qa machal...ifecnta eft eof indaf ceciderex eif illa die octe milia... Et indit eleazar filio saura una de bestus lorica...loricis rigis...erat...neus sup cetas bestias. Et infu...ei quod inca eaet xxx: & deci seuchbarer...suii adqirer s nom etnui. Et cucururie ad ea indacr imedi...uficiens aderis I asmistrus.

Although I couldn't understand a word of Latin, I had studied calligraphy at art school, and so, I painstakingly copied the manuscript from both sides of the parchment onto two sheets of paper. The Latin was almost unreadable, and contained many abbreviations and large holes (where the vellum had been badly eaten away by woodworm and death-watch beetles). Nevertheless, certain key words were legible: "elephanti," and the names "regnante demitrio" (King Demetrius), "elieazor," "bethzacharam," "capharsalama," and "timothe" (all spelt without capital initials).

I took my discovery to Canon Dobson, as I knew an elderly, parish priest at the Church of St. Mary the Virgin (next-door to the Dominican Convent in Church Lane).

A few days later he returned looking extremely satisfied with his results.

"It's a transcription from the *First Book of Macabees*, Chapters 7 and 8, and the *Second Book of Macabees*, Chapter 1," he told me. "This is printed in the Apocrypha. It's a report of the Battle of Bethzacharam, and the logistics of the armies on both sides (the number of foot soldiers, cavalry, elephants, and so on, engaged in the conflict).

Now, who would want a copy of such detailed combat information? Crusaders fighting in the Holy Land? A military order perhaps?

One of the many heresies of which the Templars were accused during their persecution in the 14th century was that they "rewrote the Bible" as mentioned in Edith Simon's *The Piebald Standard*, a reference work on the Knights Templar:

> The books were called in and many of them burned. Among those which escaped this fate, was…a volume of extracts from the Bible translated into French. (It comprised abridged versions of Genesis, Joshua, Kings, Maccabees, Tobias, Judith and Judges)…the Templar Bible consisted mainly of tales of war, and that its very existence was illegal, an act of defiance.

Presenting my discovery to The Bramston Archaeological Unit in Witham, who at the time were researching the Templars and Cressing Temple, I was met with a brief letter in reply and polite indifference. However, some years later, I discovered that during the 17th century two workmen from Witham were punished for stealing books from Cressing Temple barns. Could this page have been torn from one of these books? Did some illiterate workman, employed at the Knight Templar's house, find one of the discarded books in a nearby field and tear out a page to bind the wet clay in the cross-beam?

After we sold the house (in November of 1983), the new owners received a letter from the British Museum confirming our discovery:

> This fragment was examined, in August 1982, by the Supervisor of Western Manuscripts at the British Museum Library and was dated as a 13th century hand of exceptional skill as no single correction or erasure could be detected. It is written on extremely high-quality parchment far thinner than any available these days!

The page is almost certainly from a "service book" arranged for daily readings (as indicated by the red marginal notations showing a Friday morning and evening, and a Saturday morning). The text is taken from The Apocrypha I Maccabees, Chapter V, verses 31–68, Chapter VI verses 18–46, and Chapter VII, verses 27–68. It describes the battles in Jordan between Judas Maccabaeus, King Eupator, and the Roman, Demetrius.

Try as I might, finding a link between these 12th century warrior-monks and the Tudor house in Kelvedon proved impossible. To begin with, the dates of the house and this holy order were incompatible.

The Order of the Poor Knights of Christ and the Temple of Solomon was founded in France, by Hugh de Payns, in 1119. Bound by a solemn vow to live a life of poverty, chastity, obedience, and self-denial, the holy knights swore to protect pilgrims and roads in the Holy Land. But that was not their sole objective while in the Holy Land. As Laurence Garnder writes in his book, *Bloodline of the Holy Grail*:

By 1127, the Templar's search was over. They had retrieved not only the Ark and its contents, but an untold wealth of gold bullion and hidden treasure… (Furthermore) they were granted vast territories and substantial property across Europe, from Britain to Palestine.

In 1139, Pope Innocent granted the Templars independence, and thereby removing their need to recognize any temporal or religious authority other than the Pope. Feudalism and the ownership of land and estates throughout France, Spain, and England furnished them with money. One of those benefices was the 100 of Witham, with its parishes at Cressing, Rivenhall, and Kelvedon. The order was active for almost 200 years, made a considerable fortune, and many political and religious enemies. As Gardner writes:

By 1306 the order was so powerful that Philippe IV of France viewed them with trepidation; he owed a great deal of money to the Knights but was practically bankrupt….With papal support (Clement V, 1305–1314), King Philippe persecuted the Templars in France and endeavoured to eliminate the Order in other countries.

On March 18, 1314, by order of King Philippe IV, Grand Masters Jacques de Molay and Geoffrey de Charnay were burned at the stake in Paris. Meanwhile, in England, under the rule of Edward II, lands previously owned by the order were seized:

When this order (Knights Templar) was suppressed in 1311, Cressing Temple with their possessions passed off to the Order of St. John of Jerusalem, near West Smithfield (London).

Among the many blasphemies the Templars admitted to while being tortured was worshipping an idol—an embalmed head of the demon Bapomet—and rewriting the Bible. According to Gardner:

> In spite of the surprise effect of the arrests in 1307 and in spite of exhaustive research, the idol which thousands of prisoners confessed to having worship(p)ed—the head of wood, of silver, bearded, beardless, eyeless, carbuncle-eyed, life-sized, larger than life, the size of a fist—no such idol was unearthed.

It is believed that this "idol" may have been the enigmatic Shroud of Turin, which supposedly shows a negative image of the face of Jesus. The shroud made its sudden appearance in France, in September of 1356, following the death of Geoffrey de Charney (standard-bearer to King John II of France) at the Battle of Poitiers. The description of a face (bearded), with large carbuncle-like eyes, is quite an accurate description of the face on the shroud. Wrapped, only the face on The shroud is exposed, and when unwrapped it is indeed "life-sized." In 1978 tests used carbon dating to prove beyond doubt a that the Shroud of Turin was a 12th century fake.

Nevertheless, the Templars believed it was the face of Christ. In a Church at Templecombe, near Yeovil in Somerset, there is a painted panel matching the image on the shroud, but with large open "carbuncle" eyes.

Nearly two centuries later, in 1538, came the dissolution of the monasteries under the reign of Henry VIII. Monasteries, abbeys, and lands belonging to various holy orders were seized, and lands historically owned by the Templars (and then owned by the Knights of St. John) were confiscated a second time. But the sympathies of Henry's Catholic daughter, Mary, lay with the old religion, and she restored these lands once again (for a period of five years between 1553 and 1558). As Gardner explains:

> Queen Mary I refounded the house of the Knights Hospitallers…and granted them the manors of Witham, Purfleet, Temple-Roding, and Chingford; these, at her death, again reverted to the Crown….

Following the general suppression of religious houses, particularly of the Knights Hospitallers in 1540, the Manor of Cressing and about 50 of Witham were granted to Sir William Huse in 1541. They were then passed on to the Smyth family, who long flourished at Cressing Temple. Their ancestor was Sir Michael Carrington, standard-bearer to King Richard I during his expedition to the Holy Land.

We know from manor court records, and the writings of Thomas Wright, that during the 16th century Church Hall Manor included all the land and property in the village of Kelvedon, and belonged to the Bishop of London:

> Church Hall is so named from its vicinity to the church [of St. Mary the Virgin]. It was held under Edward the Confessor, by Angelic, one of his nobles, who gave it to Westminster Abbey…It remained part of the endowment of Westminster Abbey till its suppression…it was given, by King Edward the VI, to the Bishop of London…together with the rectory and avowson.

So, there is no direct historical connection between the house we called our home, and the Knights Templar (save for a Victorian flight of fancy in regard to the name). All the same, I had discovered a page from a Templar Bible in a Knights Templar house. The only clue as to the original builders and owners of the house was the coat-of-arms uncovered by Andrew Hamilton about 1860:

> Only one token as to date beyond the undoubted style and general character of the whole carving existed, and that exception was the supporters to a shield bearing a heart pierced with two crossed darts. These supporters were the Lion and Griffon of Henry VIII.

Basil Kentish, in *Kelvedon and Its Antiquities*, referring to the Marlers House (just across Church Lane from the Knights Templar house), mentions:

> The house eventually became the home of six "old Templars" until it was bought by the Rev. James Salisbury Dunn, who took in several boys to prepare them for college.

Today, the Knight Templar House, Kelvedon, is a Grade I Listed building.

Envied, victimized, and feared for their wealth, knowledge and power, and despite the suppression of the order, the legacy of the Knights Templar lived on. During the 16th century, in the Age of Reason, Protestantism emerged under the banner of the Red (or Rosy) Cross—adopting the heraldic symbol that the Templars changed during the 13th century. (It is significant that when the Red Cross was established in Geneva, the international relief agency identified itself by the familiar symbol.)

As Gardner points out: "the Rosicrucians (similar to the Cathars and Templars before them) had access to an ancient knowledge that held more substance than anything promulgated by Rome." Listed among the adherents to the Rosicrucian beliefs were Dante, Columbus, Francis Bacon,

Christopher Wren, and Robert Fludd who assisted in translating the King James (Authorised) Bible.

During the 16th century, the Rosicrucians were connected with Freemasonry, and in the present day the St. John's Ambulance Service (descendants of the Knights Hospitallers of Saint John of Jerusalem) is a familiar feature at many public events.

The Templars of Rousillon
By Sandy Hamblett

In the 1200s, a special detachment of the Knights Templar, known as the Rousillon Templars, came into being. This group came about at the bidding of Pierre De Voisins. Much speculation has been carried out in attempt to establish why these Templars were called in, and what they did in the realms owned by Pierre. The most enduring scenario is that these Templars either came to bury a "treasure," or to unearth one.

I would like to discuss these assertions further, and to suggest what the Templars may have been doing in regards to a "treasure."

It is true that the land that these knights occupied did have a persistent legendary association with an archaeological treasure. This treasure held the capacity of explaining the Holy Grail myths, the repeated historical references to specific families, and to the activities of certain Templar Orders.

The treasure

The main candidate for the treasure in this vicinity is that of the Visigothic King, Alaric. He vanquished Rome, and later made his kingdom in Toulouse. As Herwig Wolfram writes in *The History of the Goths*, the year usually suggested for the beginning of the Kingdom of Toulouse is 418 A.D. It is thought by some scholars that the Kingdom of Toulouse was created to preserve the ethnic identity of the Goths, who had lost their original home-land (they therefore settled permanently in the Aquitaine).

As Wolfram explains, the royal treasure of Alaric was repeatedly re-ferred to and reportedly of great significance. In fact the splendor of the Visigothic kingship was "determined by the treasure at Toulouse."

So, what was at Toulouse? It was the treasure that the Visigoths had plundered as they sacked their way across Europe. It contained coins, gold and silver, precious objects (such as the bowl dedicated to Raganhild), the riches of Rome, and the riches of Jerusalem. It also consisted of docu-ments and archives. It is usually the riches of Jerusalem which are sig-naled out as the most valuable treasure (later said to be buried in the Bézu area), and that formed the basis of a legendary treasure secreted in the Languedoc area.

If we consider the eyewitness accounts of Josephus, the Jewish histo-rian who witnessed the sack of Jerusalem by Titus, he described the trea-sures as follows:

> Now it is impossible to describe the multitude of the shows
> as they deserve, and the magnificence of them all…for
> there was here to be seen a mighty quantity of silver, and
> gold, and ivory, contrived into all sorts of things, and did
> not appear as carried along in pompous show only, but, as
> a man may say, running along like a river. Some parts
> were composed of the rarest purple hangings, and so
> carried along; and others accurately represented to the
> life what was embroidered by the arts of the Babylonians.
> There were also precious stones that were transparent…and
> of these such a vast number were brought, that we could
> not but thence learn how vainly we imagined any of them

to be rarities...those that were taken in the temple of Jerusalem, they made the greatest figure of them all; that is, the golden table, of the weight of many talents; the candlestick also, that was made of gold....After these spoils passed by a great many men, carrying the images of Victory, whose structure was entirely either of ivory or of gold.

(As quoted in *From Scythia to Camelot*)

Titus, in addition to ordering this triumphal march, also commemorated it by building a structure in Rome (now known as the Arch of Titus). There, for all to see, is that which Josephus had written down, symbolized, and preserved in stone for eternity. As one can clearly see, the Jewish Menorah and other Temple treasures are visible.

It was this treasure that Alaric got his hands on after pillaging Rome for three days and three nights in 410 A.D. Again there were eyewitness accounts to his sack of the treasure. The two following descriptions also appear in *From Scythia to Camelot*. The first, that of Orosius, is as follows:

Gold and silver vessels were distributed, each to a different person: they were carried high above the head...the pious procession was guarded by a double line of drawn swords...from every quarter the vessels of Christ mixed with the vessels of Peter.

Another eyewitness, Procopius, described as such:

The treasures of Solomon, the king of the Hebrews, a most noteworthy sight. For most of them were adorned with emeralds and they had been taken from Jerusalem by the Romans in ancient times.

It is interesting to note Orosious's comment about the "vessels of Peter mixing with the vessels of Jesus," as if they should somehow have been separated. Researchers have guessed at what these vessels were. In the case of Peter they may have included the Holy Veil of Veronica, the iron tip of the Holy Lance, and pieces of the "true cross." The holy vessels of Jesus appear to cover two items: the Holy Grail (said to be the cup he used at his Last Supper) and the Turin Shroud. The Holy Grail was equated (by Olympiodorus, in the fifth century) with the Magdalene or Marian Chalice. Originally found in the grounds of the Holy Sepulcher, it was said to have been carried to Britain during Alaric's sack of Rome. Therefore, this chalice is directly related to the Jerusalem Treasure.

This, then, is the archaeological basis of the legendary treasure of the Kingdom of Toulouse. And according to a 19th century researcher, it is this treasure that was being guarded or exploited by the Rousillon Templars. The Abbe Mazieres, in his own research, suggested the following: "It is said that the Templars exploited a certain treasure of the Visigoths, buried by them in the 6th Century, near the plateau du Lauzet, in particular Blanchefort."

If this is any way correct, it is odd that the Templars (who were formed in 1099) are said to have found something in Jerusalem during excavations they carried out under the Temple Mount. However, they could not have found the Temple treasure if it was buried near Bézu in the sixth century. This might lead to the conclusion that the Templars, if they were indeed excavating under the Temple Mount, found something entirely different. It seems Abbè Mazieres is closer to the truth when he says the Rousillon Templars were exploiting a treasure already buried. However, in the vicinity of Bézu are numerous other enigmatic villages associated with these

Templars and Templar activity. They are usually linked to the legendary treasure, and include one or more of the following claims:

- **An original and "fabulous" treasure.** This seems to correlate with the "original" Visigothic treasure. This deposit was said to have been joined at the end of the 13th Century by a new treasure from the Templar at Rousillon. This was said to have occurred on papal instruction, and perhaps relates to the excavations by the Templar under the Temple Mount.

- **The Hautpoul family secret at Bézu.** The French priest Saunière, in the course of his enigmatic excavations, seems to have impinged upon earlier Templar activity. It is well known that Saunière was said to have found a treasure at Bézu. The Hautpouls are thought to have deposited archives in their crypt at Bézu. At the time of Pierre de Voisins, who imported the Rousillon Templars to the region, Sauniere had been given lands by Simon de Montfort (at the end of the Albigensian Crusade). One of the fiefs he received was Rennes, and the Lord of Rennes at this time appears to have been Isarn d'Hautpoul. Isarn is known from Inquisition Records, as he was interrogated during the fall of Montsegur (a Cathar stronghold, said to guard the Holy Grail at the time of the Albigensian Crusade).

- **The Aniort treasure.** This is generally thought to be the same as the treasure of Alaric. It has been conjectured by some researchers that this treasure was buried in 1292. The Aniort family had strong links with the Templars in Rousillon, and provided them land and castles.

- **Sacred deposit within the domains of Rennes-le-Château.**
  This is linked to the story of Saunière, and also to the Abbé
  Henri Boudet.

- **A sacred treasure in the vicinity of Rennes-les-Bains.** This
  amazing sacred deposit, described as having a "Holy of Holies,"
  and as being dangerous to approach, appears to correlate with
  the Visigothic Treasure.

One researcher who diligently followed the tracks of Saunière has
discovered an archaeological burial. The skeleton found at this burial site
seems to have been used as some kind of a marker. Emblazoned across
the burial cloth is a large red cross, which has led some to suggest that
this find is an ancient Templar burial. If it is a Templar burial marking,
perhaps these ancient treasures may correlate with the assertion of Gerard
de Sède, who speculated that the Sauniere treasure was protected by
skeletons.

So, we have established the traditions of a treasure. Of course, it is
entirely possible that these archaeological artifacts remain. As an archaeologist, I can safely say that archaeological "treasure" is being discovered
every week. In addition, eyewitness accounts of this treasure continued
right up until the time of Clovis. In fact, as Wallace Hadrill reports of
Gregory:

> Theuderic, Clovis's son captured all the Gothic treasure
> in their capital of Toulouse, though parts of it were certainly
> in Gothic hands in Spain in the seventh century as a story
> in Fredegars chronicle, Book IV, Chapter.73 will show.
> However the Franks (the Merovingians) may have

supplemented the haul from Toulouse with more from Carcassonne including the treasure of Solomon, taken by Alaric I from Rome.

According to this account, the treasure of Toulouse had been moved and buried at Carcassonne. But prior to this, some of the treasure had been stolen by commanders in Alaric's army. (Alaric had ordered the return of the treasure to Rome, but portions of it were still missing.)

To try and grasp this more broadly, it is necessary to go back to the end of the first crusade. Readers will know that my previous research has culminated in the suggestion that the Knights Templar were created in 1099 by Godfrey de Bouillon, his brother Baldwin (who became King of Jerusalem when Godfrey died), and their powerful family advisors.

When Godfrey was made Advocatus (the king of Jerusalem in all but name), he installed some canons, along with 12 knights, into the Holy Sepulcher to protect it, and termed them the Order of the Holy Sepulcher. In 1101, an almoner of this Order was in the Lauraguais. Priests of the Holy Sepulcher also came to the Languedoc, and in 1128 Pope Honorius II, in the bull of 1128, granted 60 churches to William of the Holy Sepulcher (along with other properties in this part of Europe).

Malcolm Barber, in *The New Knighthood*, referring to the recent research by Luttrell and others, suggests that the Knights Templar were initially associated with the monks and knights that Godfrey installed. In 1120, a small group were allowed to break away from the Holy Sepulcher to form a separate group. Therefore, Barber suggests that the origins of the Templar may be found in this impetus to form a "separate" group.

This group of Godfrey's were known as "milites" (that is, men who fought on horses), and were associated with the Holy Sepulcher. The group was also known as the "milites Christ," or the "milites sancti sepulchri." It is posited that some "westerners" within the rank and file broke away to form a military order. This is all reported by Bernard the Treasurer, and collected in the accounts of Ernoul. Ernoul calls these the "earliest Templars."

Godfrey's knights and monks, drawn from the "domus godefridi" (a group closely associated with Godfrey, usually by blood ties, and constantly referred to by Albert of Aachen), were the personal retinue of Godfrey and Baldwin. They were instrumental in the election of the two brothers, and on Baldwin's deathbed they had the power to recall and vote the elder brother (of Godfrey and Baldwin)—Eustace—to become the next King of Jerusalem. (The domus godefridi were also related in some way to the Bouillon-Boulogne dynasty, and included Baldric the Seneschal, Gerard of Avesnes, Milo of Clermont, Robert of Apulia, and Herbrann of Bouillon.)

This domus godefridi supplied at least one Grand Master to the Knights Templar. If my supposition is correct—that Godfrey formed the Knights Templar through his Order of the Holy Sepulcher—then I would predict that the early Grand Masters may have had a connection to his domus godefridi. Philip of Nablus was Grand Master of the Order from 1169 until 1171. The Grand Master before him was Bertrand de Blancfort (1156–1169), and was possibly related to the Blanchefort family of the Aquitaine (if you remember Aquitaine was made the home of the Goths to preserve their ethnicity—perhaps all the ancient families which trace their lineages back to here have Gothic ancestry). Philip of Nablus's father was Guy of Milly, who was also from a prominent member of the domus godefridi.

At the Council of Troyes, where the Templar received their rule (held in either 1128 or 1129), among those present were also members of the domus godefridi, including Andrew de Baudemont, Hugh of Montaigu (the Counts of Montaigu are related to the family of Godfrey, and some members of this family were in the domus godefridi), and Master Fulcher (either the historian Fulcher Carnotensis, who was born in 1059 and later joined Baldwin I in Edessa, or Fulcherus Carnotensis, a prominent member of the Comitas Baldewini. They were both provided a crucial basis of the Bouillon-Boulogne power).

Baldwin of Boulogne was of the House of Boulogne, a cadet branch of the family of Flanders, who had descended from Charlemagne. They traced their descent right to Eustace II of Boulogne and Ida de Bouillon. The principle seat of the dynasty was the County of Boulogne. The dynasty owned St. Omer. Baldwin formed a link between the lands of Bouillon and Lotharingia, as well as that of Boulogne. He was a member of the domus godefridi, and as we have seen elsewhere, the knights of the domus godefridi helped form the Knights Templar. Is it surprising then that some of the alleged "public" founding knights were related to Godfrey, or had come from the domains that his family held?

William of Tyre tells us that "certain noble men of knightly order" presented themselves to the king, and that the most important of these were Hugh de Payns and Godfrey St. Omer. Hugh came from Lorraine, the domains held by Godfrey de Bouillon. Godfrey St. Omer came from a town owned by Baldwin I.

We also know that Andrew de Montbard, uncle of St. Bernard of Clairvaux, was one of the founders of the Knights Templar. These knights came from the Lorraine and Champagne area of France. In 1126 King Baldwin II of Jerusalem had sent Brothers (Gondomar and Andrew) to Bernard of Clairvaux in order to ask for apostolic approval and a rule. In 1127 Hugh de Payns brought a handful of Knights with him to Europe. So, who was Hugh de Payns?

Walter Map writes that a knight named Payns, from a village of the same name, had obtained from the "regular canons of the Temple of the Lord" a large house within the precincts of the Temple. He lived there poorly, and spent his time persuading and pleading with pilgrim soldiers to join up." This sounds suspiciously similar to the account given of a Knight obtaining a hall from the canons to recruit fighting men. His name was Paganus. As Michael the Syrian writes:

> At the beginning of the reign of Baldwin II a Frenchman came *from Rome* [my italics] to Jerusalem to pray. He made a vow not to return to his own country, but to become a monk....He and 30 knights who accompanied him would end their lives in Jerusalem. Identified as Hugh de Payns, the king gave them the House of Solomon to live in, and some villages.

As far as I am concerned this is still the machinations of Godfrey de Bouillon and his domus godefridi. Hugh de Payns was working among them and became the "public" face of the Knights Templar after they had been formed (at least 20 years earlier). Andrew de Montbard was followed by Bertrand de Blancfort as Grand Master of the Knights Templar.

The implication of the Blancfort/Blanchefort connection brings about all sorts of historical problems. The Abbe Mazieres reports that: "This Blanchefort/Blancfort was Bertrand de Blancfort, originally from Toulouse."

Other researchers have stipulated that the Blanchefort family were from Aquitaine—bringing us nicely back to those ancient family lineages descended from the Goths of the Kingdom of Toulouse. Mention of a Blanchefort may also be linked to a suggestion that the Commander of the Rousillon Templars was said to be a Lord Goth, whose exact identity is not clear. Speculation has included the suggestion that Bertrand de Goth (later Pope Clement V) was this Lord of Goth. Bertrand de Goth was born in Gascony in 1264, and died at Roquemaure in April of 1314. His mother is said to have been Ida de Blanchefort. He had been Archbishop of Bordeaux, making him a subject of the King of England, and was a personal friend of Philip the Fair. Bertrand studied the arts at Toulouse, and civil and canonical law at Orleans.

It was Clement V who agreed to the demands of King Philip, and ordered an investigation into the Templar Order (subsequently issuing charges of heresy against some of the members). Clement V had, however, protested against the way Philip had gone about the arrests, and he demanded that the prisoners (along with their property) be transferred to his custody. In a Bull dated March 22, 1312, Clement V said he had no "sufficient reason for a formal condemnation of the Order" (from *www.newadvent.org*). Still, he allowed the King of France to carry out his suppression of the Order.

This suppression however, did not affect the Templars of Rousillon. What was so special about the Rousillon Templars? They were based at

Le Bézu, and allegedly obtained from the Arogonese province of Rousillon.

Le Bèzu, also known as Alberdunum, which means Rochefort, was thought to have a family connection with the counts of Rochefort. There was a very early and heavy Templar presence in this land of the Cathars. They were welcomed by the Bendictine Monks of St. Mary of Alet, near Esperaza. The Templars later gained further possessions around this land. Researchers have shown that the Templars owned also the Abbey of Alet (from 1132 to 1180), and that in 1119 the Chateau of Blanchefort was owned by the Abbey of St. Gilles (a hotbed of heresy during the Albigensian Crusade). Other documents also show that around 1130 the Templars owned Peiros (Peyrolles). This was two years after the formal rule of the Templars had been granted, but it seems to me action had been going on in this area among the Templars even before their public rule had been granted.

Why was activity so strong in the area of Bèzu? There were later Templar posts and commanderies at Couiza, Rennes-les-Bains, Ruines de Aram, Bezu, as well as the famous commaderies at Douzens and Carcassonne.

After the Council of Troyes, Hugh de Payns reportedly headed for Occitania. At this time, Hugh Rigaud and Raymond Bernard were stationed there, and charged with overseeing the Order. Rigaud, for example, was hard at work in the Aude Valley, where, in the early 1130s the Templars were granted the Castle of Douzens. He also worked with the very powerful Trencavel family. (Incidentally, members of the Trencavel family held the posts of the Viscounts of Beziers and Carcassonne. The family was later suspected of being Cathar sympathizers, as they were linked to the Counts of Toulouse and the Saint Gilles clan.) Rigaud also travelled east to buy property called the "Crypt of Aiguilhe." Some records indicate that Robert of Craon—Grand Master of the Templars from 1136 to 1149—may have accompanied him on this journey.

In 1132, the Templars in Occitania met with the Trencavel clan, whereupon they were given extensive lands. Mazieres suggests that The Templars of Roussillon had conceived a grand project (the creation of a vast independent state known as the Midi). It seems obvious that certain Templar families were searching for the Visigothic treasure, their "Holy Grail."

The Templars' strong connection with the Aniort family and the Blancheforts also suggest this. Arnaud, Bernard, and Raymond de Blanchefort granted the Templars estates at Pieusse, Villarzel, and Esperaza. The Rousillon Templars settled at Bèzu and Campagne Sur Aude on land given to them by the Aniort family. Ramon d'Aniort was son-in-law to Pierre Roger de Mirepoix, and brother-in-law to Ramon de Perilla. (Raymond de Perilla owned Montsegur. Some have even identified this Perilla as the gentleman who owned Chateau Perillos, a code name used in the Holy Grail mythological cycles.)

It seems the Templars were working in the realms of the Visigoths, and were developing close connections with families whose ancestry extended back to the fall of the Visigoths (and thus may have had knowledge of the whereabouts of ancient Visigothic treasure).

Evidence indicates that there may in fact have existed two distinct treasures—one from the fifth century (consisting of tributes, taxes, and so on) thought to be stored at Toulouse, and a second cache believed to have been deposited by Alaric II (reportedly containing the ancient treasure of Jerusalem and Rome). Some of this second cache were claimed to have been discovered in the 19th Century at Guarrazar.

The treasures are discussed on the archaeological Website, *Wonders* (*http://spanish.apolyton.net/civ2/visigoths/wonders.html*):

> The Treasure found in Guarrazar (near Guadamur, Toledo) is the most important archeological finding relative to the Dark Ages. It was discovered by chance in 1855, after heavy rains uncovered the ruins of an old Visigothic city. Despite some inevitable losses, most of the Treasure has been recovered intact. The most important pieces of the Treasure are the two Crowns of Devotion bearing the names of kings Suintila (621–631) and Recesvinth (652–672).

This Website also describes the Torredonjimeno Treasure: "[This treasure was] similar to Guarrazar's. The treasure found in Torredonjimeno (Jaen) was just a depository of objects that were quickly hidden to prevent their theft by the Moorish invaders after 711. Discovered by a farmer in 1926 who did not suspect the importance of this finding, it took seven years for the scholars to become aware of the existence of the treasure. By that time, not a single piece of the collection had been left intact by the kids of the village, who had been using them as toys."

Pierre de Voisin, carving out a niche for himself after the fall of Montsegur, commandeered these lands, including the citadels at Rennes le Château and Bèzu. Surely there is a picture emerging—that Pierre de Voisin, importing the Rousillon Templars, was searching for this legendary Blanchefort/Hautpoul treasure?

The trail of that treasure goes cold in the area that the Rousillon Templars coveted. However, it begins again with Nicolas Poussin, and his painting, "The Shepherds of Arcadia" (said by some to encode the whereabouts of a huge archaeological treasure hidden in the Rennes-le-Chatea and Le Bèzu area). Is it not possible that the rest of these treasures are waiting to be found?

Schiehallion: Mount Zion in the Far North
By Barry Dunford

Biblical mysteries have perplexed many since the words were first put to paper. Among the questions that researchers still cast their speculation over include the existence of a mythological mountain, said to be the meeting place of the gods.

In the Book of Isaiah, in the Old Testament, there is a curious reference to "the mount of assembly in the far north" (Isaiah 14:13). In Gordon Strachan's *Jesus the Master Builder: Druid Mysteries and the Dawn of Christianity* (Floris Books, 1998), he comments on this biblical statement: "There was evidently a mythological mountain in the far north where the gods held their assembly."

This sacred mountain appears to be associated with "Mount Zion in the far north," as recorded in Psalm 48 in the Hebrew Old Testament. As Strachan explains:

> Commentators have pointed out that 'in the far north' cannot be a geographical description of Mount Zion [in Palestine]....Where was this other holy mountain in the north, this other mythological Zion, the abode of the gods? Was it located at Mount Meru, or the Alborg, or the Aralu, or were all these, like Mount Zion itself, pointing towards a common prototype much further north?

According to an esoteric tradition there was a primary trinity of holy mountains—Mount Moriah in Palestine, Mount Sinai in Egypt, and a mysterious Mount Heredom. The latter is not to be found on any map.

Could it be that Mount Heredom was also "Mount Zion in the far north," as recorded in the Davidic Psalm?

Isabel Hill Elder, in *Celt Druid and Culdee* (Artisan Publishing, 1990), refers to the gigantic monoliths placed in circles and piles of stones called "si'uns," or "cairns." As she points out: "The similarity of si'un with the Hebrew word 'Zion' (fortress), the Mount of Stone (as the name Zion in Celtic means) is striking."

In the writings of the Chevalier de Berage, first published in 1747, he describes the origins of Freemasonry as follows:

> Their Metropolitan Lodge is situated on the Mountain of Heredom where the first Lodge was held in Europe and which exists in all its splendour. The General Council is still held there and it is the seal of the Sovereign Grand Master in office. This mountain is situated between the West and North of Scotland at sixty miles from Edinburgh.

If we follow these directions precisely and plot a course mid-northwest from Edinburgh for 60 miles we arrive at Mount Schiehallion, which is to be found at the geographical center of Scotland.

Furthermore, Albert G. MacKay, in his *Lexicon and History of Freemasonry* (McClure Publishing, 1908) says that he found the word "Heroden" in an old manuscript of the Scotch Rites, as the name of a mountain situated in the north west of Scotland, where the first Metropolitan Lodge of Europe was held.

In a letter dated October 4, 1814, the then Deputy Grand Master and Governor of the Royal Order of Scotland states: "The Sublime and Royal Chapter of the H.R.D.M. [Heredom] was first constituted on the Holy top of Mount Moriah in the Kingdom of Judea and afterwards reestablished by King Robert the Bruce." Interestingly, after his defeat by English military forces at Methven, Perthshire, in 1306, the Scots king, Robert the Bruce, retreated into the mountain recesses of central Perthshire, where there is a strong tradition of his having taken refuge in a small castle by the north slope of Mount Schiehallion. Could this simply be coincidence?

The apparent association of the Royal Chapter of Heredom with Mount Moriah in Palestine may be pertinent when considering the Palestine based ancient Davidic tradition recorded in Psalm 48 which refers to "Mount Zion in the far north," particularly when bearing in mind the possible connection between Mount Moriah and Mount Schiehallion (Mount Heredom) in central Scotland.

The Masonic historian, George Oliver, in his work *The Historical Landmarks of Freemasonry*, volume II, (Kessinger Publishing, 2003) states:

> The only high degree to which an early date can be safely assigned, is the royal order of H.R.D.M., founded by Robert Bruce, in 1314; and very little is known about it out of Scotland. Its history in brief refers to the dissolution of the Order of the Temple....According to the testimony of Baron Westerode, who wrote in 1784, this is not the most ancient of the high degrees of Masonry.

The Rev. George Oliver goes on to say that the degree of H.R.D.M. "may not have been originally Masonic. It appears rather to have been connected with the ceremonies of the early Christians. These ceremonies are believed to have been introduced by the Culdees, (Cultores dei), in the second or third centuries of the Christian era. Operative masonry existed in Britain in that era, as is evidenced by the building of a church at York and a monastery at Iona, and it was in active operation before the 12th century."

This Celtic Culdee connection is further explained by Henry Corbin, in his address (delivered to the Eranos Conference in Ascona, Switzerland, in 1974) entitled *The Imago Templi in Confrontation* (1974) where he states:

> The primitive Celtic Church, prior to Romanization, is represented by groups of monks known as Culdees....These autonomous groups of hermit brothers correspond to what we know of the original structure of the Celtic Church...[and were]the spiritual descendants of the Essenes....It is as if the double line of descent, Hierosolymitan and Scottish, linked, *Ab origine symboli*, the Church of James and the Celtic Church in the trials and misfortunes from which the Temple knighthood have to rescue them.

Corbin goes on to further explain the Celtic connection:

> The *Coli Dei* are also included in the spiritual line of descent from the builders of the Temple of Solomon, the line of the Essenes, the Gnostics, even the Manichaeans and the Ismailis. They were established at York in England, at Iona in Scotland, in Wales, and in Ireland; their favorite symbol was the dove, the feminine symbol of the Holy Spirit. In this context, it is not surprising to find Druidism intermingled with their tradition and the poems of Taliesin integrated to their *corpus*. The epic of the Round Table and the Quest of the Holy Grail have likewise been interpreted as referring to the rights of the *Coli Dei*. It was, moreover, to the time of the *Coli Dei* that is assigned the formation of the Scottish knighthood whose seat is

typified by the mysterious sanctuary of Kilwinning, under the shadow of Mount Heredom in the extreme north of Scotland.

An esoteric tradition tells of a Templar Knight named Robert of Heredom, who, after being initiated in a cave on Mount Carmel, came to Scotland. In support of this tradition, Crobin comments on the "Sons of the Valley," who he identifies as: "an exalted company of initiate Brothers, who constitute *ab origine* the secret Church of Christ."

Corbin goes on to further state:

> Robert of Heredom is thus initiated by the Sons of the Valley and created Grand Master of the new Temple, which will be born again from the ashes of the old....Robert's name in chivalry refers us to the mystical mountain of Heredom in the north of Scotland....The entire Scottish tradition is thus evoked, the part played by Scotland in the renaissance of the Order of the Temple after its destruction. The person of the young knight likewise comes to be integrated to the *geste* of the knights who, in the company of Pierre d'Aumont, were accorded in Scotland the protection of King Robert the Bruce and, according to the tradition, continued the Temple there.

Furthermore, as Oliver informs us:

> The Temple Masons were bolder: they met on the summit of Mount Moriah. These knights, says the "Encyclopaedia Metropolitana," were much connected with the Masons, and are supposed to have been frequently initiated among the Syrian fraternity. On the dissolution of their Order, in

the 14th century, the Provincial Grand Master of Auvergne, Pierre d'Aumont, with two Commanders and five Knights, fled, disguised as Masons, to one of the Scottish isles, where they found the Grand Commander, Hamptoncourt, and other members of their Order; and they resolved to preserve the institution, if possible, although in secret, and adopted many of the forms of the Freemasons, to conceal their real designs. They held a Chapter on St. John's day, 1313, when d'Aumont was chosen Grand Master; and in 1361 their seat was removed to Aberdeen.

According to tradition the Scottish isle in question was the Island of Mull.

The conical Mount Schiehallion ("the fairy hill of the Caledonians") has long been considered a sacred and mystical mountain by the gaelic Highlanders of Scotland. Its topographical features are somewhat reminiscent of Mt. Shasta (in California) that is held sacred by the North American Indian tribes.

In his classic work *Cuchama and Sacred Mountains* (Swallow Press, 1981), the Buddhist scholar W.Y. Evans-Wentz comments:

> In the scriptures of mankind, certain mountains are considered sacred; and they are referred to as being sources of inspiration and revelation to prophets, saints, and sages. Mountains rising on high and merging into the invisible depths of space come to be looked upon as being the abodes of heavenly beings, the repositories of wisdom, and the founts of spiritual illumination.

Evans-Wentz goes on to say (speaking about Mt. Omei, a sacred mountain in China):

Phenomena of most unusual character are associated with this Sacred Mountain, and at least some of them may merit a more than purely mundane explanation. The monks and pilgrims who frequent Mt. Omei believe these phenomena to be self-evident proof of its sanctity.

Geographically, Mount Schiehallion is located at the very center of the Scottish mainland. Similarly, we find the sacred hill of Uisnech at the geographical centerpoint of Celtic Ireland, and also the five-peaked mountain called Plinlimmon sited at the center of Celtic Wales. Can this really be a geographical coincidence?

In Hugh MacMillan's book *The Highland Tay* (H. Virtue, 1901), he comments on Mount Schiehallion, saying that it is a "well-preserved glacial monument, which speaks impressively of the great icy tool that sculptured its sphinx-like form...it is a residual, adamantine knob of pure quartz." He further remarks: "It is the spire of the whole vast landscape, lifting it up to heaven, and giving it something of the feeling of poetic or religious awe which, from the earliest time, the human mind has felt in the neighbourhood of great mountains."

John Sinclair in his work entitled *Schiehallion*, published in 1905, writes:

Schiehallion is distinguished as a widely known and very beautiful mountain....I envy not the man who can climb Schiehallion without experiencing certain emotions of reverential awe, which raise the thoughts of the heart from earthly to heavenly things. I can truly say that in my climbings of the dear mountain, I invariably felt myself, as it were, in a sweet atmosphere of Bible imagery, thinking of Moses, Elijah, the Saviour, and others, when they climbed those sacred mountains in the east, and there held communion with the great Father of spirits.

The following curious story related by Robert MacDonald (a former minister of Fortingall) in the new *Statistical Account for Scotland* (Perthshire, 1845), may be relevant to the theme of this article:

> There is a very remarkable cave near the south-west angle of *Sith-chaillinn* [Schiehallion], at the 'Shealing,' called *Tom-a-mhorair*, or the Earl's eminence. Some miles to the east, there is an opening in the face of a rock, which is believed to be the termination thereof. Several stories are told and believed by the credulous, relating to this cave; that the inside thereof is full of chambers or separate apartments, and that, as soon as a person advances a few yards, he comes to a door, which, the moment he enters, closes, as it opened, of its own accord, and prevents his returning.

It is interesting to note that the same minister comments that the local people "may be characterized as intellectual, sober, and industrious in their habits, honest, and religious."

Moreover, in *Rambles in Breadalbane* (T. Murray, 1891), the author, Malcolm Ferguson, when writing about Mount Schiehallion, remarks: "It is said that there are a long series of mysterious caves, extending from one side of the mountain to the other." (Interestingly, the Masonic historian and researcher, A.E. Waite, mentions three Templar Knights who found refuge in "the caves of Mount Heredom.")

It has often been recorded that many of the ancient esoteric orders and mystery schools held initiation ceremonies in caverns and underground grottos. As Oliver informs us:

…in some of the philosophical degrees, the place of meeting is figuratively termed a cavern, in imitation, probably, of the spurious Freemasonry, which was always held in the bowels of the earth; and the most stupendous specimens of the fact are visible to this day in the Indian, Persian, and Egyptian subterranean temples. In some places, entire mountains were excavated, and the cavern was constructed with cells, chambers, galleries, and streets, also supported by columns, and forming a subterranean labyrinth. Examples of this practice are found in the excavations underneath the great pyramid of Egypt; at Baix and Sena Julia in Italy; near Nauplia, in Greece; at Elephanta and Salsette, in India; at Ceylon; and in Malta is a cave, where we are told that 'the rock is not only cut into spacious passages, but hollowed out into numerous contiguous halls and apartments.' Similar cavern temples are found in every country upon earth.

Donald A. Mackenzie, in his work *Buddhism in pre-Christian Britain* (1928) remarks: "In Scotland various caves lead to the Underworld." Could this be the case with the mysterious "Tom a Mhorair" (the giant's cave), located on the south west flank of Mount Schiehallion?

A similarly mysterious cave is to be found on the giant mountain Ben Mhor, having a circumference of forty miles, that is located on the Scottish western Isle of Mull. In *The Riddle of Prehistoric Britain* (reprinted by Health Research, 2003), Comyns Beaumont writes:

Ben Mhor possesses two unusual features. One is a series of rising terraces towards its summit which may have been natural or roughly made by man. The other is the enormous cavern at its west base looking to the open Atlantic, known as MacKinnon's Cave, with which many eerie legends are connected. Some believe it was a pagan temple to a seagod, and this finds support from the fact that an inner cave possesses an ancient and immense flat stone, perhaps part of a former cromlech, called Fingal's Table, but some think was a pagan altar and sacrificial stone. Local superstition keeps visitors away, added to the fact that the sea enters the cave and flows far inland with the rising tide, for it is said that the cave's recesses pass right through the mountain to the other side.

Further pertinent information is to be found in *A Highland Parish or the History of Fortingall* (1928), where Alexander Stewart comments:

Schiehallion is in a special sense the mountain of myth and mystery....At the west shoulder of Schiehallion is Creag-na-h-Earra, with its covering of heather and boulders and its base laved by two burns. At the point at which these two burns meet is situated a rock that bears more cup marks than any other stone surface of the same size in the British Isles. Near the same place is...Tom a Mhorair....Some miles to the east of this there is another opening, which tradition holds to be the other end of the cave. According to the traditional accounts, this cave was regarded as an abode of fairies and other supernatural beings, rather than a hiding place of mortals. The only men who were supposed to have lived there were individuals who were believed to have been in league with supernatural powers.

Could the foregoing be indicative of the mysterious Mount Heredom, the high abode of spiritual adepts, which the Old Testament Prophet, Isaiah, knew as the holy "mount of assembly in the far north," and the King David knew as "Mount Zion in the far north"?

While the mystery of the mountain may continue, the spiritual sanctity of Mount Schiehallion is captured in the following poetry:

> *O! if there be on earth a Paradise,*
> *Where righteous souls in glory wait in trust*
> *Till the sweet resurrection of the just,*
> *Methinks that region round Schiehallion lies,*
> *And that good angels, hovering o'er its cone,*
> *Impart to it that chaste and heavenly tone.*
>
> *I love to view Schiehallion all aglow,*
> *In blaze of beauty 'gainst the eastern sky,*
> *Like a huge pyramid exalted high*
> *O'er woodland fringing round its base below;*
>
> ....
>
> *The Bible tells of Hebrew mountains grand,*
> *Where such great deeds were done in days of old,*
> *As render them more precious far than gold*
> *In our conception of the Holy Land;*
> *But every soul that seeks the heavenly road*
> *May in Schiehallion, too, behold a Mount of God.*

—From "Schiehallion," by John Sinclair

One Possible Source for the Grail: The Joseph of Arimathaea Connection
By Mark McGiveron

I will here posit an argument that many of the apocryphal legends about Joseph of Arimathaea come from misappropriated stories found in Old Testament works, and from the writings of Flavius Josephus.

Perhaps the most enduring legend about Joseph of Arimathaea is of his connection with the Holy Grail. The first person to make the link between Joseph and the Holy Grail was the French poet Robert de Boron, in his prose romance *Joseph d'Arimathie* (or *Roman de l'estoire du Graal*), written about 1190.

In Robert's story, the Holy Grail is the cup or chalice used by Christ at the Last Supper. Joseph subsequently uses it to collect the blood of the crucified Christ at the Deposition (when Jesus is taken down from the Cross). These two factors seem to imbue this cup with intense sanctity, and make it an immensely magical relic. Later Robert writes "When on the third day, the Jews discovered that the body (of Jesus) was missing, they accused Joseph of stealing it and threw him into a dungeon."

While Joseph was in prison, the crucified and now resurrected Christ supposedly appeared to Joseph "in a blaze of light" and presented him with the sacred chalice and told him that he was to be "the guardian of the vessel." Christ also instructed Joseph in the symbolism of the mass, and informed him that the vessel containing the divine blood was to be called a "calice."

Joseph was later freed from his imprisonment and voyaged to Britain with the "calice," or Holy Grail.

Robert de Boron's romance largely influenced the development of later Grail legends (most notably the Vulgate Cycle, that was probably composed by monk(s) who, similar to Boron, presented a very "Christian" Holy Grail to their readership). But the question remains: What texts and accounts fed into Boron's composition?

There is one source which, many scholars agree, Robert used to create his own work. This is a fourth century text variously titled the *Acta Pilati* or *the Acts of Pilate*, but more often referred to as *The Gospel of Nicodemus*. In the Middle Ages it was a very popular text (as attested by the number of medieval copies still in existence, and the number of languages in which it was printed).

The Gospel of Nicodemus is the major source of early, noncanonical information regarding Joseph of Arimathaea. Large sections of Robert's *Joseph d'Arimathie* correspond to it (although in *The Gospel of Nicodemus* there is no mention of a grail or cup of any kind). This raises the question as to why Robert incorporates the element of a cup or chalice in the legend. Does Joseph of Arimathaea simply supply him with a narrative device on which to hang the story of a Holy Grail onto? I don't think so. Rather, I believe Robert found a connection between Joseph and cup or chalice somewhere else. Additionally, I believe this source can be identified.

In my opinion the story of Jesus presenting the Chalice to Joseph of Arimathaea has been appropriated, or rather, misappropriated, from stories about the life of an earlier Joseph. In this case, it was "Joseph of the coat of many colors," as presented in Genesis 30: 23–24.

This Joseph became the favorite son of his father Jacob, despite being the youngest of his 11 sons. After Jacob gave Joseph a garment of many colors, the other sons became jealous. When Joseph later tells them two dreams, that clearly portend to his future elevation over them, the brothers come to despise him. As they fed their father's flocks in Dothain, in the land of Canaan, they seized Joseph, took him to Egypt, and sold him into slavery.

Joseph becomes the property of a rich Egyptian noble man, and was well treated. That is, until the wife of the noble man attempted to seduce Joseph. When he turned her down, she accused him of those very criminal solicitations which she had herself committed against him.

In Genesis 39:19 it is written: "His master hearing these things, and giving too much credit to his wife's words, was very angry."

It is at this point that I believe the stories about this old testament Joseph start to run curiously parallel to the apocryphal legends of Joseph of Arimathaea. It is necessary to reiterate here that the legends of Joseph of Arimathaea—as expressed earliest in the Gospel of Nicodemus, but also Robert's *Joseph d'Arimathie*—have Joseph of Arimathaea being cast into prison by "the Jews" (*The Gospel of Nicodemus*) after the Crucifixion.

The Genesis account (39:20), referring to the earlier Joseph, continues as follows: "And (His Master) cast Joseph into the prison, where the king's prisoners were kept, and he was there shut up."

Shortly afterwards, two of Pharaoh's officers (the chief butler and chief baker), having incurred royal displeasure for some reason unknown to us, are locked up with Joseph. When they are troubled by clearly visionary dreams Joseph kindly interprets them. It is the chief butler's dream that is of import to this investigation, as this dream makes mention of a cup: "And the cup of Pharaoh was in my hand: and I took the grapes, and pressed them into the cup which I held, and I gave the cup to Pharaoh." (Genesis, 40:11)

However, I do not believe Robert de Boron knowingly borrowed the cup motif from the chief butler's dream in the book of Genesis. The book of Genesis was readily available to all medieval scholars, making any misappropriation from this text impossible to make accidentally. Such knowing misappropriation would have been scurrilous, and I do not believe a good Christian such as Robert would sink to such a depth. But misappropriation from a separate commentary upon the same story is quite feasible.

How could such a thing happen? Well first it is necessary to remember that even many of the greatest medieval libraries were not as comprehensive as any of our contemporary local town or district libraries. There was, by today's standards, a limited amount of material available to the inquisitive scholar. Also, those who consulted the available texts did not have as developed a sense of historicity as most modern readers. This can be illustrated by the fact that medieval scholars illuminated their manuscripts with biblical representations of characters, fashions, and landscapes based on their own time and location. Thus, Pharaoh is portrayed as a medieval king, and Roman soldiers as medieval foot soldiers and knights.

So, bearing this in mind, I ask you to imagine the following scenario: A monk, for the sake of narrative lets call him Hugh (although Urbino or Guillermo would be just as appropriate), is making notes from a manuscript at a monastic library. Hugh is a guest at the monastery, and he is making notes for the monks of another monastery. Perhaps he is also not very intelligent. He copies down a passage from a manuscript about Joseph's life in prison. Maybe he is in a hurry, or maybe he is just sloppy. For some reason, however, he makes an error of narrative placement.

Could this have really happened, and could this ultimately have led to Robert de Boron's account of Joseph receiving the Holy Chalice or cup from Christ while in prison? If w consider the following paraphrase of a first century account, to my mind the best candidate for such a misappropriation, this possibility does not seem so farfetched.

The following passage is taken from *The Antiquities of the Jews*, by Flavius Josephus. It is a commentary on the Genesis account of Joseph's (son of Jacob) imprisonment in Egypt.

What things befell Joseph in prison

In his sleep Joseph saw three clusters of grapes hanging upon three branches of a vine, all ripe for gathering. He squeezed them into a cup which the king held in his hand, and when he had strained the wine he gave it to the king to drink. He received it from him with a pleasant countenance.

Reading this passage Hugh might have recognized the name Joseph. To Hugh, the squeezing of the grapes into the cup clearly represents the chalice of the sacrament and the wine of the last supper. Also, in the Gospel of John 15:4–7, Jesus also refers to himself as the vine. Perhaps having recently read *The Gospel of Nicodemus* Hugh believes Josephus to be talking about Joseph of Arimathaea, and therefore entitles his transcript *What Befell Joseph of Arimathaea in Prison*. This would accentuate his awry interpretation even further.

This transcriber, perhaps Hugh, perhaps not, puts two and two together and gets five—not uncommon in the field of historical study. Indeed one could say, with absolute certainty, that a large amount of biblical analysis is based upon misinterpretation, misrepresentation, and presumption.

Were the Templars Head Worshippers?
By Oddvar Olsen

The tragic attack on the Templar Order by Phillip the Fair of France has been imprinted in the human psyche by the date of their arrest—Friday the 13th. A resurgence of interest in the Templar Knights was created by Dan Brown's *The Da Vinci Code*. As we know, his book is fiction.

Similarly, many scholars throughout the centuries have claimed that the accusations created by Phillip and the Inquisition were also fictitious. For example, the Templars were accused of worshipping a head, or head-like idol. However, if we consider the medieval accounts from the trial, and some of the different theories put forward in later years, perhaps some sense can be made of this and similar accusations.

Here is the list of charges the Inquisition drew up against the Templar:

- The knights adored a certain cat that sometimes appeared to them at their assemblies.

- In each province they had idols, namely heads (some of which had three faces, and other only one) and human skulls.

- They adored these idols, especially at their assemblies.

- They venerated these idols as representative of their God and savior.

- The Templar said that the head could save them and provide them with riches.

- The idols had provided all of the Order's riches.

- The idols made the land germinate and the trees flower.

- They surrounded or touched each head of the aforementioned idols with small cords, which they wore around themselves next to the shirt or the flesh.

- During one's reception, the aforementioned small cords (or some length of them) were given to each of the brothers.

- They performed all of their activities in veneration of their idols.

The previous account is taken from Malcolm Barber's *The Trial of the Templars*, and Barber has also included a description of how the Templar's idols may have looked. Although not many of the Templar brothers have described the idols in the same manner, below are some extracts from the Parisian hearings that provide us an idea of the head-like idols:

- Brother Raul de Gizy "had seen the head in seven different chapters, some which were held by Hugues de Pairaud, the Visitor. When it was shown, all those present prostrated themselves on the ground and worshipped it. It had a terrible appearance, seeming to be a figure of a demon, known in French as 'un maufe.' Whenever he saw it, he was filled with fear, and he could scarcely look at it without trembling. However, he had never worshipped it in his heart."

- The same Pairaud confesses that he has "seen, held, and stroked it at Montpellier in a certain chapter, and he and other brothers present adored it. He said however that he had adored it with mouth and for the purpose of feigning, and not with the heart; however, he did not know if the other brothers worshipped with the heart. Asked where it was, he said that he sent it to Pierre Alemandin, Preceptor of Montpellier, but did not know if the king's people had found it. He said that the head had four feet, two at the front part of the face and two at the back."

- Etienne de Troyes describes the head as "flesh from the crown to the shape of the neck, with hairs of a dog and without any gold or silver covering, indeed a face of flesh, and…very bluish in colour and stained, with a beard having mixture of white and black hairs similar to the beards of some Templar."

- Other Templars questioned following Jean de la Cassagne claimed to have seen an idol, the bearded head of the figure of Baphomet, a wooden black and white idol called Yalla (a Saracen word).

- Brother Stephen de Troyes stated that he saw a head in the Paris chapter, and he claimed it was the head of Hugh de Paynes.

The previous examples are some of the most vivid descriptions, but they didn't stop there, as some brothers said the head had two faces, and others claimed three. Still others described the idols as ancient embalmed heads with "hollow, carbuncled eyes, glowing like the light of the sky." The colors of the head(s) varied as well, from white to blue, to red, brown, and black.

The different testimonials must be considered in the light of fact that they were obtained under severe torture. Understandably, many people would say anything to please the ears of the dreaded "Holy Roman Inquisitions."

According to John de Dorrington, during the trial in England an old Templar had told him that the Order was in the possession of four principal idols. One was housed in the sacristy of the Temple (in London), another at Bristleham, a third at Temple Bruer, and a fourth at a place beyond the Humber (Yorkshire). What those idols were is not clear. It is possible that the panelled "head" painting at Templcombe (in Somerset) may have been one of them; especially when you consider that Bristleham is also known as Bristol, and that the panel painting was brought to Templecombe for safe keeping. (In 1945, the painting was accidentally discovered—it had been concealed beneath the plaster of an outhouse at a Templar manor.)

King Edward II had been very reluctant to imprison his allied Templars, and after he had, he was hesitant to subject them to any torture. When he finally arrested the Templar (some three months after Phillip the Fair had swept his devastating hand across France), hardly any confessions were made. Nor were any artifacts of a heretical nature discovered. This is not a big surprise—if the Templars had been in possession of any unorthodox artifacts, they would have had plenty of time to secrete them after they became aware of the arrests of their fellow brethren in France.

In addition to the previous evidence, there were several contemporary medieval legends that alluded to head worshipping. These narratives often concerned a man, sometimes a Templar knight, who was in love with a lady. During their lifetime they are never to be together. The tales take a bizarre turn after the woman dies. The man digs her up and has intercourse with her deceased body! Some accounts also claim that he then cut off her head. Then, after nine months had passed, the man returned to the grave. Once again, he dug up his beloved lady—this time he found a human head between her legs. This head had miraculous powers of different sorts, and sometimes resembled those of the Holy Grail or the Ark of the Covenant. (Barber outlines further details of these legends in his text.)

In later years, there was speculation that the Templar followed John the Baptist, and may have been in the possession of his decapitated head. (Many books have been written upon this subject, so I will not discuss it in great detail.)

In the late 1800s, occultist Eliphas Levi popularized the image of the androgynous, horned Devil/Pan.

Levi interpreted the word Baphomet by reversing it as follows: "Tem omp ab." He thought this was a Latin abbreviation of "Templi omnivm hominum pacis abbas," or in English, "The Father of the Temple of Peace of all Men." Levi believed this referred to King Solomon's Temple.

Some commentators believe the Baphomet is a corruption of Muhammed, because the Templars were in contact with various Muslim sects (they converted and became Muslim heretics). However as it is against Islamic faith to have idols, this seems very unlikely indeed. Other historians think it is a corruption of the Arabic term, "Abufihamat," meaning "Father of Understanding," or "Father of Wisdom," which was the Sufi terminology for God. Those leaning towards the notion that the Templars were in possession of and worshipped the Baptist's head explained it as follows: Baphomet was derived from two Greek words, "Baph," and "Metis," meaning "Baptism of Wisdom."

Baphomet. From private collection of Oddvar Olsen.

Hugh Schonfield, a biblical scholar and one of the first to translate the Dead Sea Scrolls, also believed that the Baphomet referred to wisdom. He came to his conclusion by using the ancient Hebrew Atbash Cipher. (A method of decoding language, the Atbash Cipher involves substituting the first letter in the language with the last. So, for example in English, A=Z, B=Y, and so on.) Schonfield, in his work *The Essene Odyssey* (Element Books, 1993), explains his theory as follows:

> Setting down Baphomet in Hebrew characters produced, which by Atbash converted immediately into "Sophia" (the Greek word for Wisdom). So this centuries old secret was for the first time revealed! But what about the bearded

male head? In the cosmic figure Admon Kadmon (Sky Man) the bearded male head is denominated in Hebrew as (Chokmah), that is, Wisdom. The Greek Sophia represents a female rather than a male, and we are not surprised to find in Templar hands, according to Inquisition records, a casket surmounted by "a great head of gilded silver, most beautiful, and constituting the image of a woman."

The next obvious question is: Did the Inquisition find any evidence of head worshipping within the Templar Order? The simple answer is yes, they did. In *The Knights Templar: a New History*, (Sutton Publishing, 2001), Helen Nicholson writes: "The Draper of the Order and two knights stated that during the trials of the Order in Cyprus that they had never heard of any idols in the Order, but the Order had the head of St. Euphemia."

After the dissolution of the Templars, the head of St. Euphemia was passed on to the Knights Hospitaller. Nicholson in her book speculates that it ended up in Malta with the rest of the Hospitaller's relics, and was stolen by Napoleon's plundering troops. (It is currently today said to be housed in the patriarchal church of St. George, in Istanbul.)

Another head was also found in the Paris Temple, rumored to be that of the legendary Caput VLIII. The royal custodian, Guillaume Pidoye was asked to search the Temple at Paris after Guillaume d'Arrebley The Preceptor of Soissy admitted he had seen a silver head on the altar during chapter meetings. Pidoye went searching for this head, and as Barber explains, after several weeks he produced:

A certain large beautiful silver-gilt head, shaped like that of a woman, within which were the bones of a single head, rolled up and stitched in a certain white linen cloth, red muslin having been placed over it, and there was sewn in there a certain document on which was written 'Caput LVIII,' and the said bones were considered as similar to the bones of the head of a small woman, and it was said by some that it was the head of one of the eleven thousand virgins.

After this head was produced, Guillaume d'Arrebley told the Inquisition that this was not the head he had seen; in his original statement he described it as a doubled-faced bearded head.

Again, as with the head of St. Euphmedia, the Templars were clearly venerating heads, but for what purpose is unclear.

Though the debate will likely continue as to the purpose of the knight's veneration (whether it was as devoted Christian soldiers innocently worshipping one of their many Christian relics, or as sinister worshippers of Baphomet), we can at least acertain with some certainty that they were worshippers of heads.

Templar Preceptories

Templar Sightings in Bristol and Somerset
By Oddvar Olsen

Within the United Kingdom, Bristol and Somerset were of major importance to the Knights Templar, with Bristol and Templecombe as the most recognized sites of Templar activity. As I traveled through Somerset looking for Templar evidence, to my delight I found a Templar tomb slab at Montacute, and further Templar curiosities in other places. In considering the Templar's legendary activities in these two areas, I think it is possible to further ascertain whether there is any truth to the accusations that the Order worshipped head-like idols.

Templar evidence in Bristol

The parish church of Holy Cross overlooks Victoria Street, in what was the first suburb of the old city of Bristol. It lies to the south of the river Avon, and the church can easily be recognized by its leaning tower.

Holy Cross, Bristol.
Photo by Oddvar
Olsen.

This Templar church, despite its strategic location, was not a preceptory, but was compromised to Temple Guiting in Gloucestershire.

It was Robert, the Earl of Gloucester (son of Henry I), who gave the Templars the land in Bristol. Bristol's Templar church was founded in about 1145, and representative of the Templar's first architectural building phases (signified by a round or oval church). The church was hit in the air raids of November 24, 1940, and only the footings remaining.

According to the accounts of both a Minorite Friar and John de Dorrington, the Templars had four principal idols which they worshipped (one at London, in the sacristy of the Temple, another at Bristelham, a third at Temple Bruer, and a fourth at a place beyond the Humber (Yorkshire).

Bristelham could be either Bisham or Bristol. If Bristelham is Bristol, as George Tull claims in his *Traces of The Templars* (The King's England Press, 2000), then it is possible that the panel painting found at Templecombe had been transported from Bristol for safekeeping.

Templar evidence in Somerset

Templecombe is found among the lush Blackmore vale in Somerset. In 1185 Serlo Fitz Odo granted what would become the one and only Preceptory of the Templars in Somerset. It was here, in the manor that (in 1945) a Mrs. Drew (the tenant of Mrs. A. Topp) discovered the panel painting that had puzzled scholars for years. Drew had gone to the outhouse, since demolished, to collect wood for the fire. She happened to look up at the ceiling and discovered that some plaster had started to peel away.

When investigating this further, she saw a face looking down at her. The painting had been tied with wire into the roof and concealed by plaster.

Thanks to the generosity of Topp and Bishop Wright (the rector at that time), the painting was saved and donated to Templcombe's St. Mary's Church in 1956. It can today be viewed on the south wall in the church. St. Mary's was built as a daughter house to the great Benedictine Abbey at Shaftsbury. It is be-

Panel painting, Templecombe. Photo by Oddvar Olsen.

lieved to have been founded soon after 888 A.D., by Ethelgeda, the daughter of Alfred the Great.

The oldest parts of the existing church are a 500-year-old nave wagon roof, a transept with piscine, and a Purbeck Marble font. As with Holy Cross at Bristol, St. Mary's was directly affected by the German air raids of World War II—three bombs destroyed most of the old church.

Let us now return to the panel painting for a moment. The panel painting of a head is one of the finest examples of its kind from the medieval period. The life-sized painting has been carbon-dated to 1280.

There have been numerous theories put forward regarding its origin. Some people have claimed it is a copy of the Turin Shroud. However, this strikes me as very unlikely. The image on the Turin Shroud shows a man with closed eyes, while on this painting, the person pictured has his eyes open. Unfortunately the top portion of the panel is missing, but it does not appear to have included a halo. (A halo would have been portrayed over the head if this were a picture of Jesus the Christ, God's son.) During the suppression of the Templars, the inquisition used the absence of a halo in the Templars' pictures of "Christ" as evidence of idolatry. (They were also accused of worshipping a head of varying descriptions. The last Grand Master of the English Templar knights was William de la More. We know he had been at Templecombe during the interrogations of the Templars, as one William Raven describes his reception at Templecombe, with William de la More as Master.)

Until the suppression of the Templars, the main responsibility of the Templecombe Preceptory was to admit new members and train men and horses for the crusades. Sheep farming seems to have also played a part in the day-to-day life of the Templars at Templecombe, as the Templecombe Templars purchased 20 acres of land for 1,000 sheep (and 60 other beasts) to pasture on a few miles north at Temple Haydon (today called West Harptree), near Templecloud. (Wool was needed in great quantities to make white robes for the Templars in England and on the continent.) A 1383 inventory shows 368 acres of land belonged to the Templecombe Preceptory.

During the Templars' trials John de Dorrington also admitted that an elderly Templar had told him that the four idols were introduced to England by William de la More. (William was one of the few Templars in England who refused absolution. As was the case with many of his French brethren, he was prepared to die for the cause. He claimed complete innocence, and died in the Tower of London in February of 1311.) Did the French Templars know what was to come? Their fleets were communicating between the ports of Bristol and La Rochelle on the French coast. Perhaps the four icons had been sent from France to England for safekeeping?

Templar curiosities

Skull imagery can be found in many areas with Templar lineage. For example, in the village of Stoke-Sub-Hamdon the graveyard of St. Mary the Virgin contains carvings of skulls and crossbones on at least two of the old tombstones.

The symbolism of skulls rings familiar. In Golgata (the place of the skull) we've heard mention of St. John's head on a platter. Additionally, many more references to heads have shown up in the Arthurian romances. And the Freemasons keep 200 odd skulls in the Grand Lodge in London. Similarly, graves from the 13th and 14th century Knights Templar have been found with their legs taken off and crossed on their chest, just beneath the skull.

In St. Mary's Church at Shapwick there are a number of Templar crosses in the churchyard, and a few more inside the church. In addition, there is the very elaborate tomb of Henry Bull Templer Strangeways decorated with skulls and crossbones. Strangways' tomb dates from the 19th century, and is probably of Masonic origin. (His name suggests some sort of a strange Templar connection, and may be worth further investigation.)

If one travels further, to Brent Knoll (just a north of Burnham on Sea) and the church of St. Michael, there are several 15th century church pews. On one of the pews is a wooden carving of the Agnus Dei, the Lamb of God, who is looking back over its left shoulder and gazing at a decapitated head.

Church Pew, St Michael's, Brent Knoll. Photo by Oddvar Olsen.

A very similar head can be found in Alford, near Castle Cary (again, on a pew as at Brent Knoll). This pew features a dragon encircling a head. There is also another Agnus Dei in the church, which is seen looking back at a decapitated head. What do we have here? I will let the reader make up his own "head"!

Church Pew, Alford Church. Photo by Oddvar Olsen.

There is an old Templar legend about the "Skull of Sidon," recorded by Walter Map in the 12th century. It claims that a Templar knight had a relationship with a woman who had died. He dug up the woman's corpse and consummated their relationship, which resulted in a most grisly birth nine months later. As J.S. Ward states in *Freemasonry and the Ancient Gods* (Kessinger Publishing, 1997), the legend is as follows:

A great lady of Maraclea was loved by a Templar, A Lord of Sidon; but she died in her youth, and on the night of her burial, this wicked lover crept to the grave, dug up her body and violated it. A voice from the void then bade him return in nine months time for he would find a son. He obeyed the injunction and at the appointed time he opened the grave again and found a head on the leg bones of the skeleton (skull and crossbones). The same voice bade him "guard it well, for it would be the giver of all good things," and so he carried it away with him. It became his protecting genius, and he was able to defeat his enemies by merely showing them the magic head. In due course, it passed to the possession of the Templar order.

At the entrance of St. Mary's the Virgin, in Stoke-Sub-Hamdon, there is a fine Tympanum showing figures of Sagittarius, a lion, and an Agnus Dei. Agnus Dei is said to represent St. John the Baptist, one of the patrons of the Templars. The most accepted explanation of this Tympanum is that Sagittarius represents King Stephen of England (the elder brother of Henry de Blois), and the lion represents Stephen's cousin Geoffrey of Anjou. (These two were bitter rivals competing for the throne in England at that time.) Stoke-Sub-Hamdon lies six miles south of Leo, in the Glastonbury Zodiac, that historian Katherine Maltwood claims was refined by the Knights Templar.

Some time ago, I was invited by Gordon Geard (a scholar and writer of the history of Montacute) to visit him in Montacute. While there, he proposed a stroll around this delightful village in Somerset. After visiting St. Catherine's Church, we went outside and he told about how one of the churchwardens had upset him by placing a bench over an ancient tomb slab. Smiling, he told me I might find this one interesting.

As I investigated the ancient tomb slab closer, I could distinguish a sword engraved on the top of it. At that time, I was in the process of reading *The Temple and the Lodge*, by Michael Baigent and Richard Leigh, and remembered their mention of

Possible Templar tomb slab, Montacute. Photo by Oddvar Olsen.

the graves they had discovered in Kilmartin that were engraved with "a stark unadorned image of swords." (I later visited another former Templar church, St. Michael's Church in Garway (Herefordshire) and found more confirmation of the use of swords engraved on the top of Templar tomb slabs, perhaps as an insignia for high-ranking Templars.)

Perhaps the high-ranking Templars chose anonymous graves, instead of big monuments and elaborate decorations, to show that they had renounced the pretensions of the material world.

As mentioned in Chapter 4, Henry de Blois maintained certain connections with the Templars. It was in Montacute that Henry was appointed Prior of the Cluniac monastery in 1120. This monastery, as was the case of so many other places, came under the influence of King Henry VIII. And also similarly, not many remain. (We do not know much about the old monastery at Montacute because no proper excavation has so far been executed. Hopefully this will be done one day.)

There were only four Templars in Templecombe when the Order was suppressed. The fate for the English Templars was quite different from their brethren in France. Only a few years in a monastery was enough for absolution. We know one of the Templars from Templecome came to serve his sentence in the Benedictine monastery at Montacute, under the supervision of Henry de Blois.

When excavating the tomb of Henry de Blois at Winchester Cathedral, a small ivory head and a chalice were discovered. What we have here are two of the sacred objects that figure so strongly in the Templar myths: the Chalice or The Holy Grail, and the head the Templars were accused of worshipping. Keith Laidler in *The Head of God*, suggests that not only was John the Baptist decapitated, but that Jesus was as well, and that the Templars were in possession of their decapitated heads.

I hope, based on what I have presented so far, that we can at least start to understand the importance of the Holy Grail imagery and influence in Somerset. Despite the fact that the Templar only held one preceptory in Somerset, the area cannot be underestimated.

Balantradoch: The Scottish Temple
By Bob Mander

I first visited Rosslyn Chapel in the early summer of 2000. In doing some preparatory reading for the visit, I came across *The Temple and the Lodge*, by Baigent and Leigh, and the reference to Temple, near Rosslyn. This temple was subsequently added to my itinerary.

Prior to my visit, the inquiries I made regarding Temple were responded to, on numerous occasions, by the simple reply: "it's sacred." This was enough to inspire my journey, and I set off with a sense of anxious anticipation.

Temple, Scotland, viewed from East. Photo by Bob Mander.

The journey proved interesting, as it revealed links between the Templars and the Hospitallers (the Knights of St. John of Jerusalem and Malta), it further emphasised the links between the Templars and the Masons—thus providing a glimpse as to why the site is sacred to both the Templars and the Freemasons.

While not much compares to the particular atmosphere of Rosslyn, Temple has special "air" all its own. The peace and tranquillity that greets you as you enter the graveyard is unmatched.

Interestingly, the link between the Templars and the Hospitallers has been highlighted in the new edition of *Bloodline of the Holy Grail* (Fair Winds Press, 2004), where Laurence Gardner reveals that in 1307 Robert the Bruce set up an Order known as the Elder Brethren of the Rosy Cross. The Order contained senior representatives from both the Templars and the Hospitallers. It is interesting to note the date in this case (also one of the earliest references to the Rosicrucians). The Stuarts eventually took the concept to London when they ruled over both countries. This eventually led to the establishment of the Royal Society in the 17th century with a predominance of Rosicrucian members.

(Please note: In the course of the research for this article, three different spellings of Balantradoch were found, with Ballantradoch and Balantrodach being the other variants. The most commonly encountered spelling has been used throughout.)

The History of Temple

The year 1118 is the generally accepted date for the establishment of the Order of Poor Knights of Christ and the Temple of Solomon—later shortened to the Knights Templar (although Baigent, et al, develop a very persuasive argument that the Order was founded at least four years earlier in *Holy Blood, Holy Grail*). Although Hugh de Payns was the nominal founder of the Order, it is likely that more significant figures, such as the Counts of Anjou and Champagne amongst others, provided the incentive for the foundation of the Order.

It seems clear from numerous modern accounts that the Rex Deus families, sometimes called the desposyni (as outlined by Gardner in *Bloodline of the Holy Grail*)—namely the bloodline descendants of Jesus (sometimes called the underground stream)—had very clear motives for wishing to return to Jerusalem. It was members of these families that caused the Templars to become established.

In 1128, Hughes de Payns arrived in Britain as part of a major "recruitment drive" for the Templars. He had been well received in France, and had gained numerous adherents and lands (he was similarly received in both England and Scotland). As *The Anglo-Saxon Chronicle* states:

> He was received by all good men, and they all gave presents to him; and in Scotland in like manner. And moreover they sent to Jerusalem great wealth in gold and silver. And he invited people out to Jerusalem, and there went along with him and after him so many people as more had never done before since the first expedition during the days of Pope Urban.
>
> (As quoted in *The Scottish Review*, July 1898)

In Scotland, Hughes de Payns, who had been married to a member of the St. Clair family before forming the Templars, found particular favour with King David I (by all accounts, a devout man). The Abbot Aelred of Rievaulx, writing about the king, had this to say:

> [He] entrusted himself entirely to the guidance of religious (monks), retaining beside him the most noble brethren of the distinguished military order of the Temple of Jerusalem, he made them both by day and night custodians of his morals.

King David awarded the Templars the village and lands around Balantradoch as the site of their first and main preceptory in Scotland. (Balantradoch can be translated as "the settlement of the warrior." While the Templars in Britain were primarily governed from the main Temple in London, and Balantradoch remained subordinate, it nevertheless became an important center of the Templars in Scotland, as is evidenced by the following, from *The Scottish Review*:

> At the same time, although in this strict subordination to England, the Scottish Templars had a chief of their own who was usually styled the Master, but sometimes the Preceptor, of the House (or Knighthood) of the Temple in Scotland—Magister Domus (vel Militiae) Templi in Scotia—and who had his headquarters at Balantradoch in Midlothian, the principal house of the order to the north of the Tweed. The name Balantradoch has long ago vanished from the map of Scotland, but the significant name of Temple, which has succeeded it, and which designates the modern parish wherein the preceptory and its lands were situated, is the most notable vestige of the order that Scottish geography has to show. The ruined church of Temple, which stands picturesquely on the banks of the South Esk a few miles above Dalkeith, is of a later date than the dissolution of the order, and apparently there are now no remains of the Preceptory, although from a tradition rather vaguely reported by Augustus Hay, it seems that "the foundations of a vast building and the root of several big pillars of stone" were discovered at some time in the seventeenth century, in a garden in the neighbourhood.

The names of the Preceptors, or Masters, have not been preserved as an accurate list, but the ones who are known seem to be mainly of English or French descent. The names that are known include Bartholomew, Robert of the Temple, Ranuelph Corbet, Hugh de Conyers, Roger de Aikney, Brian de Jay, John de Soulre, John de Huseflete, and

Brother Walter de Clifton. In truth there were not many knights of the Order actually based in Scotland, and most members belonged to the second or third ranks—namely chaplains (capillari), or serjeants (servientes armorum). Many of the knights who served as preceptors over the years were men of great experience, who, either because of age or injury, were unsuited to serve the Order in other ways.

The main site was located near the South Esk river, on a small terrace next to the river. This site included the aforementioned preceptory, a church, a mill, and a large dovecote. Incidentally, a conversation with the owner of the old manse situated next to the church elicited the information that significant stonework had been discovered around the its foundations. This, presumably, was part of the remains of the preceptory, and seems to confirm the information contained in *The Scottish Review*.

At the time the Templars resided here, the main occupation appears to have been farming, as there were a number of serfs living in small cottages within the village. The serfs were expected to give time to tilling, farrowing, and so on, on the preceptory lands. The Templar would also have reared some animals, and some would have worked in the mill on the opposite bank of the South Esk grinding corn.

It must be remembered that Balantradoch was located in the middle of the St. Clair lands, and would have received considerable support from that family. There was also close links with another preceptory on the south side of the river Dee, at what is now the modern parish of Maryculter. Of course, the preceptories were not the only lands under the control of the Knights Templar—they were given the rights to many manors and other estates. Most of their possessions in Scotland were in the Lothians—namely the area to the south of Edinburgh on the eastern side of the country.

In 1308, following the "official" dissolution of the Templar order by Pope Clement, the Preceptory at Balantradoch was given to the Knights of St. John. This handover actually took place because this part of the country was under the control of the English at the time. The Knights of St. John substantially rebuilt the church into a more traditional rectangular shape, and the preceptory buildings gradually fell into disrepair. But otherwise, life seemed to carry on in much the same way as it had under the Templars.

With regard to the dissolution, it is worth noting that the two Scottish knights, Brother Walter de Clifton and William de Middleton, were examined by the Bishop of St. Andrews and Papal Chaplain John Solario at the Church of the Holy Cross in Edinburgh concerning the so-called misdemeanours of the Templars. This examination elicited nothing of either a criminal or heretical nature. Throughout the rest of Scotland, very little seems to have happened as a result of the dissolution of the Order. England and Scotland were at war, Robert the Bruce had been excommunicated, and the end result was that a large number of Templar knights fled to Scotland to avoid persecution. These knights came from the Scottish borders, England, and a large number from the Continent (on board the Templar fleet). It is now generally accepted that a significant force of Knights Templar took the field on the side of Robert the Bruce at the battle of Bannockburnm, and thus played an important role in the defeat of the English.

Prince Charles Stuart was elected Grand Master of the Order in 1745, and he remained so until his death in 1788, even though he and most of the Templars had fled to France after the battle of Culloden in 1745. It was in this period that closer ties with the Masonic order, already underway as early as the late 15th century, gathered pace—and has continued to the present day.

Johnston Stephen writing about Temple in the *Cockpen Bazaar Book* (1897) states: "In one of De Quincey's papers there is elaborate examination of theories that have been advanced by different writers concerning the Templar's rituals and practices, some of them seeking to show that the ritual of the Freemasonry of today is a survival of, or has in it vestiges of, that which belonged to the Order of Templars." The same author makes the point that late in the 19th century there were still current documents referring to the Templars holding land.

After the Act of Reformation in 1535 (under the rule of Henry VIII), the Knights of St. John lost their control of Balantradoch. The church was enlarged to make it more "suitable" for Protestant worship, and a gallery was added at the western end. In 1618, Balantradoch had its name changed to the Parish of Temple, when it was combined with the ancient parish of Clerkington and the chapelry of Morthwait (also known as Muirfoot, or Morphet). The church then remained in use until the 18th century, when a new church was built near the property.

The Reverend James Goldie, at the end of the 18th century commented on the declining numbers in the parish. Between 1723 and 1733, they averaged 31.5 baptisms a year, 6.5 marriages, and 33.5 funerals. Between 1784 and 1794, they averaged 15.5 baptisms a year, 1.5 marriages, and 16 funerals. The decrease in numbers is very evident. The population at this time were still primarily engaged in "farming and pasturage."

The old Parish Church, Temple

The church is a simple rectangle, with the inside measuring approximately 55 feet long and 17 feet 9 inches wide. Most of the present structure dates from after 1312, when the Knights of St. John were granted the title to Balantradoch by Pope Clement V (following the suppression of the Templars). The church is on the site of the Templar church and, no doubt, parts of the present structure date from the 13th century.

After the Reformation (1535), the Knights Hospitaller were dispossessed in their turn, and the Church had to be made "suitable" for Protestant worship. Some 17 feet were added to the western end, including a gallery along the west wall with a high-level access door. At the same time the slightly incongruous belfry was added at the east end and two other side doors to the church.

In the original building, the five windows remain. The aesthetically pleasing east window dominates that end of the church. The north and south walls both have two fine traceried windows, although the western one in the north wall has been blocked off, with some evidence of it showing in the interior. In addition, there are two narrow lancet windows in the north and south walls, near the west end of the original building. All these windows have hoods terminated with carvings of roses.

On the north wall, close to the trefoil-headed sacristy door, there is a small arched area, now largely derelict, thought to have been the Easter sepulcher. Nearly opposite, on the south wall, are the remains of an arched sedilia—this was a seating area for two people, each space having a trefoil shaped arch over it. A piscina, now in poor condition, is also located in this area. This was a basin with a drain used for the washing of hands at appropriate times during the services.

The older part of the church has some fine buttresses setting off the building to good effect. These are grouped on the east and south sides of the church. Similar buttresses were to be found on both the north and south walls, but there are now only the two remaining in the south. It is possible that the cut stone (ashlar) from the missing buttresses was used in the construction of the west end of the church.

The gable ends of the church are also of interest. The older, eastern end has had the belfry added, and there is evidence of the wear in the stone caused by the bell rope. Beneath the bell space, on the right-hand side there is an inscription in the stone—not filled with lead—and is thought to represent the following Latin initials:

VAE SAC IMI. H.M

Belfry, Temple, Scotland. Photo by Bob Mander.

Some historians have interpreted this inscription as ancient Roman writing rescued from a preexisting site, but it seems more logical that this is a later inscription (possibly dating to the period when the Knights Hospitaller took contriol of the site in 1312). The *Illustrated Architectural Guide to Midlothian* (1995) interprets the inscription as:

Vienne Sacrum Militibus Johannis Hierosolymitani Melitensibus

This translates as: "The Sacred Council of Vienna to the Knights of St. John of Jerusalem and Malta."

A later translation (2001) was proposed by researcher Jeff Nisbet, who thought that it was associated with the Templar belief in the holy bloodline descending from Jesus and Mary Magdalene, and perhaps to the voyage of Henry St. Clair to America.

Beneath this stone is a round, heavily-weathered sandstone boss set in the wall, the significance of this is hard to detect. The "newer" gable at the western end is surmounted by a Templar cross, presumably rescued from the site and set in place when this section was erected.

At the eastern end of the north wall, there are two items of interest. Beneath the window there is a heavily weathered tomb from the late 14th century and, next to it, but higher up the wall, there is a projecting weather-table (indicating that there was perhaps a monument, tomb, or even a sacrament house at this point).

MacGibbon and Ross date the main body of the church to the late 14th century, although an earlier date would have been ascribed except that: "In Scotland allowance must be made for backwardness" (*The Ecclesiastical Architecture of Scotland*, 1896). It seems likely, however that a much earlier date can be assumed. The same authors also state that the church "is valuable as an example of the decorated period in Scotland, of which few, if any, parish churches are now to be found."

The Graveyard

The graveyard is situated in a beautiful wooded area, in a loop of the South Esk river. It is bound by high walls to the north, east, and south, and by the old manse—with its walled garden—to the west. The graveyard itself and the church are on a flat, low-lying area (although bounded by terraces to the east and south). It is shaped as an irregular quadrilateral, roughly 200 feet from west to east, and a similar dimension from north-west to southeast.

The graveyard has short, well-tended grass, and is a haven of peace and tranquillity—justifying its description of "sacred" by Templars and Freemasons alike. There is a seat located near to the entrance where it is a delight to sit and meditate on a pleasant day.

There are numerous gravestones in the graveyard. They mainly date from the late 17th and 18th centuries, but there are some older stones in the cemetery that have been missed by some authorities. These are mainly to be found on the terrace in the south-east corner. Some of the stones in the main area may also be a little older, as they have a Templar "feel" about them.

The graveyard does clearly show the links that can be established between the Templars and the Masons. Inside the church there is a "modern," 20th century stone showing a Templar influence. On the east wall of the church there is a monument to Charles Kitchener (1831) of the Stobs Mill gunpowder works.

Recent developments

Work is ongoing in the area around the old churchyard to discover more about the Templar occupation of the site. A groundscan of the land attached to the Old Manse, now a private house, has been undertaken, under the auspices of *Pharo.com* and Radar World Ltd. (of the Elvinstone Science Centre, near Edinburgh). The funding for the scan was provided by Niven Sinclair. The project has the twin aims of discovering more about this important Templar site and evaluating the efficacy of new technology in studying such historic sites.

As the *Pharo.com* Website explains:

> Radar World's ADR (Atomic Dielectric Resonance) system is a development of conventional radar technology

that enables the operators to detect not only the presence of objects underground but also to determine the substance of which they are composed. This is a significant advance on current ground-scanning techniques, such as Ground Penetrating radar, which can only indicate the presence and approximate size and shape of subsurface artefacts.

For the first time, ADR allows a detailed "slice by slice" visual presentation of what lies beneath an area of ground to be built up. Buried objects, cavities and other anomalies can then be identified for digging.

The system has obvious advantages that are noninvasive, comparatively cheap, and flexible.

The scheme commenced in December of 2001, with a series of vertical and horizontal scans being eventually completed. These were used to draw up a composite picture of the grounds of the Old Manse. The results of the ADR scan are being used to draw up plans for series of concentrated excavations of the site to determine the true extent of the Templar holdings there. "The ADR system identified several possible graves and metallic objects, along with various interesting subsurface structures that appear to be walls and arches, beneath the grounds of the Old Manse." There is also the possibility of a tunnel and stone steps on the site.

Postscript

In varying degrees, we can all feel the spirituality of sites such as Temple, Rosslyn, Melrose Abbey, and also the great ancient places such as Avebury, Stonehenge, Castlerigg, Carnac, and the Giza Plateau. It is something that we feel within us, in our heart's center.

Temple has been described as "sacred" by Templars and Freemasons. As with Rosslyn, it is obvious that there are also links between the two groups. It is not just that they have both used the sites, but rather that there is something about the sites that have caused them to be so used—they are centers for the light of spirit.

Visiting these sites should be seen as part of a journey that we are all making. It is a journey of personal discovery, of enlightenment. Such a journey is always more pleasant if you travel with like-minded friends, but we must never lose sight of the fact that we are on a personal voyage. We are striving to reach the same goal but on different pathways. What we each see, feel, and experience may well be different, for we are all seeking our own Holy Grail. The Grail stories of the 12th and 13th centuries were all about individual, personal journeys of discovery.

So, in visiting Temple we are taking a step on our own search for the Holy Grail. In summing up the wonder of Temple, one can simply say that there is far, far, more there than the sum total of its immediately apparent parts.

St. Michael's Church, Garway
By Oddvar Olsen

Nearly 10 miles south of Hereford, alongside the river Monnow, lays the Church of St. Michael. The old Templar preceptory site is difficult to find today as it sits gently nestled in this green and fruitful valley. To be sure, it was much more difficult to reach than in 1180, when the land was granted to the Templars by King Henry II. Surrounded by tall trees, hidden away, veiled in mystery, it gives a feeling that it is hiding something.

This Templar perceptory at Garway (or Llangarewi, as it was called in the past) was a very important place for the Templars on the Welsh border.

St Michael's Church, Garway.
Photo by Oddvar Olsen.

Approaching the old Templar site, the massive tower of St. Michael's Church (33 feet square, 70 feet high, and with narrow windows), its defensive purposes become very clear. When walking toward it today, however, it radiates a feeling of comfort, peace, and tranquility. It must have been an ideal place for the Templars. Of its history, we know that the last Grand Master of the Templars, Jacques de Molay visited the Garway preceptory in 1294 (making it one of the few preceptories in England that received the honor).

Malcolm Barber, in *The Trial of the Templars*, tells us of a Templar priest named John de Stoke. While being interrogated, he gave an account of his meeting with Jacques de Molay. A year after John's orthodox reception, John was called before Jacques de Molay and other Templar brothers. Jacques had asked John "…in whose image the crucifix was made?"

John replied, "It was of Jesus Christ."

De Molay then threatened to take John to prison because "…he (Jesus) was the son of a woman and since Jesus said that he was the Son of God, he was crucified."

Asked by the Inquisition what Jacques had told John to believe, he explained that he was told to "deny Christ, but believe in the great omnipotent God, who created heaven and earth, and not to believe in the Crucifixion."

Only two people were arrested at Garway during the suppression, William de Pokelington, and Philip de Mewes (the last Templar Grand Master at Garway). Philip was tortured and charged with heresy—in the end he admitted to false beliefs and publicly confessed.

If you visit St Michael's, there are several curiosities to look for. Let's first consider some of the "graffito" carved in the stones on the outside wall of the Church.

The grafitto has been carved in different types of stones, so they do not appear to be from the same time period, or crafted by the same hand. (Also, these stones are not consistent with the majority of the other stones used to build St. Michael's.)

In 1927, the footings of the original Templar church were found on the north side. It is a fine example of the Templar's first building phases, similar to the examples to be seen at Templechurch in London, and Holy Cross in Bristol.

The east window is decorated with two carved heads that look out upon the surrounding landscape. The one on the right-hand side is known as "The Dead Man's Face," and is similar to the strange heads inside Templechurch in London.

The Dead Man's face, St Michael's Church. Garway. Photo by Oddvar Olsen.   *A Grand Master with a Mitre, Garway. Photo by Oddvar Olsen.*

The one on the left-hand side is called "A Grand Master with a Mitre," and was perhaps meant to be a dedication to Jacques de Molay following his visit there.

The inside of the church offers a surprising splash of interior decorating, as the walls are covered in a horrid lilac and light pink. When I first entered the church I felt like someone had played an "inquisitive" joke on us. As my vision got used to that color I realized that even more historical desecration had occurred. Walking eastwards towards the High Altar I found myself standing on a Templar tomb slab, or rather, half of a tomb slab: the Templar grave had been broken to be used as chancel steps. There was also another one used as rood stairs. Perhaps someone understood that the Templars were a major stepping-stone in history! And there is still another Templar tombstone used as a window lintel.

After the shock I decided that I had better sit down on one of the old wooden church pews to rest my broken spirit. I finally got my breath back, and let my eyes wander upwards in prayer.

Green Man, Garway. Photo by Oddvar Olsen.

With great relief, I found my eyes looking at a beautiful blue-barrel ceiling, decorated with 24 golden, six-pointed stars. Once again, the feeling of tranquility and serenity returned to me.

On the top of the pillars leading into the chancellery there are two curiously carved figures. One of them is the famous "Green Man," with foliage flowering out of his mouth.

Just below the Church there is a very fine dovecote built in the latter days of the Templars. The inscription above the entrance tells us it was built by "Brother Richard." This Columbarium lies on the site of the original Templar preceptory (since demolished). Parts of the manor were still visible in 1844, but were removed for what is now a farmhouse.

The dovecote is one of the finest in this country and possibly one of the most peculiar as well, with the curious number of 666 pigeonholes in 19 rows. You can only ask yourself whatever gave the Templars the idea of embedding this much-debated number in the hatching place of their doves.

Dovecote, Garway.
Photo by Oddvar Olsen.

The Fall of Acre: The Last Battle for the Holy Land
By Stephen Dafoe

With the death of Bohemond VII in October of 1287, the rightful heir apparent of Tripoli was Bohemond's sister Lucia, who resided in Italy. The leaders of the area wanted no part of an absent ruler, and offered the helm to Sibylla of Armenia, who accepted (and later tried to install Bishop Bartholomew, whom the Templars held in great contempt for earlier political issues). While this decision of the rightful heir met with strong objections from local leaders and merchants, Lucia would not back down. The people of Tripoli decreed that the royal line was deposed, and that Tripoli would be a commune, as had been the case in Acre.

Sometime in 1288, Lucia arrived in Tripoli to assert her claim on the land. However, the new commune did not want to relinquish its newfound power of self-rule. The leaders petitioned the Genoese to make Tripoli a protectorate. This was well received by the Genoese, as they welcomed the addition of an important trading partner. War ships were immediately dispatched to defend the city from any forces Lucia might send.

The Venetians backed Lucia, and the Templars (allies of the Ventians) offered their support. Soon after, a mysterious envoy of Christians arrived at the door of Sultan Kalaun in Egypt, requesting that he intervene in the turmoil brewing in Tripoli.

The envoy was mysterious in that the names of those in attendance were not recorded, although some historians suggest that the Templar Grand Master, and certainly the secretary of the Order, were aware of whom they were. The argument presented by the envoy was that if the Genoese gained control of Tripoli, Egyptian trading in Alexandria would be seriously impaired.

This news met with great approval in the court of Kalaun, as he had been looking for an excuse to break his treaty with the city. Although the Templar Grand Master was certain of Kalaun's motivations, he could get no serious audience in Tripoli, where everyone seemingly had an unswayable faith in the treaty with Kalaun.

In March of 1289, de Beaujeu's words were finally accepted, but it was far too late. Some 10,000 Moslem soldiers had already surrounded the city. The Venetians and the Genoese had galley ready, and were quick to evacuate their people to Cyprus.

Tower after tower began to fall to the steady beat of Moslem war drums, as catapults pelted the walls. The Venetians were the first to flee, followed soon after by the Genoese (both taking all the supplies their galleys would hold). The remaining citizens were paralyzed with fear as the ships had gone to sea, taking with them their only visible means of escape.

When news of the exodus reached the ears of Kalaun, he moved with great haste, as he knew that the Italians would load their galleys with the richest of materials ahead of their own people (and he had desperately wished to plunder the city of its merchandise). Thus he ordered an immediate assault, in order to halt the further shipment of goods.

As the Moslem army stormed the walls, they were met with only mild resistance, because Almaric of Cyprus had fled the city with four galleys (loaded with his own army, the Templar marshal De Vanadac, and Lucia). De Modaco was left in charge of the remaining Templars, and was slaughtered along with the few remaining Christian forces that tried to save the city from the invaders.

When those fighting in the streets were killed, the armies of Kalaun began going house to house, killing the men and sending women and young boys off in shackles to be sold as slaves. When the city was occupied they set off to do the same on a small island, where some had fled in small fishing boats.

After all was said and done, Kalaun ordered the walls of the city leveled. After that destruction, Tripoli effectively ceased to exist. The Templars were devastated at having lost such a sizable contingent of men (which, in light of the events to come, they could scarcely have afforded to lose).

Back in Acre, the citizens were in shock at the loss of Tripoli. They had falsely assumed that their trading status with the Moslems would assure them a position of safety. King Hugh immediately dispatched word to the Pope and the collective monarchs of Europe requesting military support. The support was not to be forthcoming, and the collective opinion was that there was not a strong enough need for a new crusade to defend the Holy Land.

Support did eventually come (in the form of a small army of mercenary soldiers—consisting mainly of unemployed Italians and peasants). As the Venetians had a vested business interest in Acre and an excellent fleet of ships, they transported the unskilled and untested army to Acre.

However, when they realized that no pay was forthcoming for their efforts, the untrained army began to rob the citizens and steal from the merchants. One morning a street fight broke out between the soldiers and a group of Moslems. History does not record the cause of the fracas, but it soon led to a full-scale riot as more and more people took sides in the fight. At the end of the day many Moslems lay dead and the families of the slain wanted revenge and justice.

An envoy of mourners left Acre for the court of Kalaun. On arriving they were given audience with the sultan, and each one in turn told his or her version of the tale. Kalaun vowed justice, and immediately prepared every siege engine he had available, and set his army out to deliver the needed punishment. Kalaun did not, of course, make this decision public. Instead, he sent letters to the Christians demanding that the guilty be turned over to him for proper trial.

The Venetians, who had brought the army to Acre, were vehemently opposed to this. Their opinion was that it would reflect badly on them to simply turn the men over to the Moslems. Although long-time allies with the Venetians, the Templars took the contrary view, and felt the men should be turned over to the sultan if peace was to be restored and Acre was to remain safe.

De Beaujeu, the Grand Master of the Templars, knew the sultan's motivations and was chastised by the Christians of Acre for being a coward. The citizens felt the Templars were more interested in protecting their growing financial interests, and had given up their original role as protectors of the Christian faithful. In this sense, they felt the Templars had turned their back on Christ.

The Grand Master's warning was not heeded, and letters were sent back to the sultan. These letters expressed deep regret for the unfortunate incident, and laid the blame on the guilty Venetian soldiers (and not at the Kingdom of Jerusalem). While the Christians were using political spin to save their hides, Kalaun was building a formidable war machine. Word began to trickle through Outremer that war was afoot. To divert their attentions from his true goal, Kalaun circulated a story that his war machine was destined for the Sudanese and Nubians, who were both late in their tribute payments.

De Beaujeu did not believe the deception for a moment and continued to warn Acre, but his warnings fell upon deaf ears. As the Grand Master had not given his support to the Venetians, the Venetians sought to get even by not lending their support to the Templars.

An envoy of Templars was sent to Kalaun, who thought it was the city he was interested in (and not the people who lived there). The people of Acre could all leave and take what they pleased, but the price would be one gold sequin per head spared.

When the envoy returned, the Templar Grand Master called a meeting of the leaders to explain what he felt was Kalaun's fair and affordable proposal. He was again called a coward. The people of Acre were insulted that De Beaujeu would have them surrender their homes (and pay for the privilege of doing so). If they paid the ransom for their exodus there would be no funds to defend the city, and surely the Moslems would kill them out of pure revenge for those who died in the riot that started the whole mess.

The cards dealt by Kalaun were of little importance, because by the time any decision had been made, Kalaun lay dead in his tent, having never heard the outcome of the Christian's decision. This did little to stop the ultimate fate of Acre, as a new player picked up the cards his father had dealt. Al Ashraf Khalil was ready to carry on what his father had begun. The siege engines were built, swords were sharpened, and horse hooves shoed. However, winter had fallen so it was decided that the advancement of the army would wait until spring.

Meanwhile, the Christians at Acre were anxious to learn the intentions of the new sultan and sent an envoy of one Templar, one Hospitaller, an Arab translator, and a secretary. As soon as they arrived they were jailed. Word later came back to Acre that they were dead.

In the spring of 1291, the sultan's army began its invasion. The citizens of Acre, who during the previous fall had so chastised the Grand Master of the Templars for his cowardice, now begged him to save them from the coming army.

While the Templars held the largest force in Acre, and the Hospitallers also had a good-sized army, they were no match for the 160,000 invaders. The Templars and Hospitallers, always at the ready to wage war, set out to make preparations for the coming battle. The Teutonic Knights, who also had a force in Acre were politically ridiculed and embarrassed when their Grand Master resigned in fear of the coming battle. However, they were able to elect a new leader in time for the battle.

The Genoese loaded their vessels and left before the fighting started. Having nothing to gain from the war, and not wishing to aid the rival Venetians, they saw no fit reason to stick around.

A great wall surrounded Acre at the time, supported by 10 towers. Although this would seem a secure fortification, it was only a temporary means of protection against the many siege towers and catapults the Moslems brought with them.

Because the sultan did not send a fleet, the seaside was open to the Christians for supplies. One ship was quickly equipped with a catapult and set to sea to protect the city from any fleet that might come forth.

On April 6, 1291, the first volley from the catapults began. As the battle raged on the Templars quickly became discouraged by their role as mere defenders. They had nearly two centuries of attack experience, and didn't like being on the receiving end of one. They soon decided to launch an attack on the Moslem's camp under the cover of darkness.

One evening, the St. Lazarus Gate quietly opened, and the silence was replaced with the hoof beats of 300 Templar war horses tearing into the Moslem camp. Unfortunately, the darkness meant to provide cover did not provide the Templars with enough visibility. The horses tripped on tent ropes and the fallen Templars were slaughtered where they stood, further depleting their forces, which were already vastly outnumbered by the enemy.

Ever the rivals, the Hospitallers set out to show the Templars how to do the job, and on another evening they charged off under the cover of darkness from the St. Anthony Gate (which was in their quarter) to finish the job the Templars had started. This time the Moslems decided to throw a little light on the issue, and they set the brush afire.

The Hospitallers seeing there was no chance of success beat a hasty retreat back through St. Anthony's Gate. Thus ended the nightly forays into the sultan's camp.

With each passing day, the walls cracked more and more, as volley after volley rang out from the Moslem catapults. By May 16th, one tower had cracked, and the invading army was able to enter (forcing the Christian's back to the inner wall of the doomed city). Clearly they were losing valuable ground in their defense of Acre. Two days later the sultan ordered all the kettle drums to sound, and the thundering beat of the advancement was disheartening to the trembling people of Acre.

Khalil ordered the forces to storm the walls and deliberately attacked all sides simultaneously, further spreading and weakening the Christian's defenses.

With this attack came the death of the Grand Master De Beaujeu. As thousands of arrows were shot over the walls, one met an unprotected area of the Grand Master's armor. As he was carried away, the crusaders begged him to stay and press on. His response was that he could do no more, he was already dead. True to his own words, De Beaujeu died within the day from his fatal arrow wound.

As the battle waged on the Hospitaller quarter was the first to be breached, and as the Moslems stormed the wall, the St. Anthony Gate was quickly opened (allowing more soldiers through). Soon after, the Hospitaller Grand Master received a wound, but continued to fight on. He had to be forcibly removed by his men, and was sent off to sea.

Seeing the writing on the wall, many began to flee. Almaric left in his vessels and took many nobles with him. Otto de Grandson, the Swiss leader fighting for Edward I, loaded his English army into Venetian vessels and set off to sea as well. The rank and file citizens fought for possession of anything that would float, and also set off to water.

As was the case in Tripoli, the men were killed and women and young boys shackled as slaves. The army then plundered the city.

Those who could escape made their way to the Templar fort at the southernmost tip of the city, where there were approximately 200 Templars remaining. Rather than fleeing, they had vowed to stay and protect the women and children who had sought refuge in the Temple. (Of course not all Templars were so valiant. Roger de Flor commandeered a Templar galley and offered safe passage to anyone with the prerequisite financial remuneration for the voyage.)

Some five days passed as the Templars held the women and children in the safety of their fort. Annoyed that this one remaining building was obstructing the defeat of the city, Khalil sent an envoy to make a deal with the Templars. If they relinquished the fort, the lives of the women and children would be spared and the Templars could take with them not only their weapons but all they could carry.

Peter de Severy, the commander of the last remaining Templar fortress in Acre, seeing no other possible solution to the stalemate, quickly agreed to the terms. The castle gates were opened and the Moslems entered and hoisted the sultan's banner. But contrary to the deal that had been made, the Moslems quickly began molesting the women and young boys. This outraged the Templars, who felt they had been lied to.

The doors of the castle were quietly closed and barred, and swords were silently drawn out of their sheaths. In true Templar fashion, they slaughtered all of the attackers. The sultan's flag was hoisted down and the Beauseant replaced. The battle was resumed and the garrison of Templars shouted that it would continue on until their very deaths.

That evening, under the cover of darkness Tibauld de Gaudin, the Temple's treasurer, was escorted into the fort. He loaded the Templar treasure and as many women and children as he could onto his ship and set sail for the Templar castle at Sidon.

The following morning the sultan sent an envoy to the fort and they expressed their deepest regrets for the actions of a few guilty men. This was a similar situation that had once been offered to the sultan by the Christians to save Acre before the battle ever began. The envoy said that the sultan wished to meet with the commander of the fort to offer his personal apologies, and to ensure that the surrender terms would be upheld this time.

Peter de Severy, it seemed, had not learned a lesson from the earlier dealings with the sultan. He selected a few Templars to accompany him on the trip to the sultan's camp. Once the party was outside they were brought to their knees and beheaded as their slack-jawed fellow knights watched from the walls of the fort.

The sultan's miners continued to work on the foundations of the fort, and when all was ready they set timbers ablaze. As the walls began to crack, Khalil ordered a party of some 2,000 soldiers to storm the fort. The added weight of the attacking forces on the crumbling structure was too great, and the entire building collapsed (killing not only those who were inside, but those who were trying to get inside).

With the destruction of this last Templar stronghold, Khalil's conquest of Acre was completed. Meanwhile, de Gaudin (the treasurer) received word that he had been elected the new Grand Master of the Order. He immediately loaded the treasury and set sail for the island of Cyprus, the main headquarters of the Templars (and an island they had once purchased from Richard I). He vowed to send reinforcement troops, but these troops never surfaced.

As city after city fell to the Moslems, the Holy Land slipped from the hands of Christendom. All that remained of the Templars in the Holy

Land was their castles at Tortosa and Athlit. On August 4, 1291, Tortosa was abandoned, and less than two weeks later Castle Pilgrim at Athlit was left unoccupied. Thus ended Christendom's hold on Outremer, and the Crusades were effectively brought to a close.

It is ironic that although the Templars were the last to give up the fight, they were ultimately blamed for the loss of the Holy Land. These accusations would feed a growing contempt for the order, and hasten their ultimate demise at the hands of a king destined to capitalize on their growing unpopularity.

Freemasonry

A History of Canadian Masonic Templarism
By Stephen Dafoe

Much has been written over the years about the formation of Masonic Templarism. Indeed, some authors contend that Freemasonry evolved out of the dissolved and persecuted Templars of old. This theory is not new as the chevalier Ramsay, in his famous oration of 1730, also painted a crusader pedigree upon the Masonic fraternity:

> At the time of the Crusades in Palestine many princes, lords, and citizens associated themselves, and vowed to restore the Temple of the Christians in the Holy Land, and to employ themselves in bringing back their architecture to its first institution. They agreed upon several ancient signs and symbolic words drawn from the well of religion in order to recognize themselves amongst the heathen and Saracens. These signs and words were only

communicated to those who promised solemnly and even sometimes at the foot of the altar, never to reveal them. This sacred promise was therefore not an execrable oath, as it has been called, but a respectable bond to unite Christians of all nationalities in one confraternity. Some time afterwards our Order formed an intimate union with the Knights of St. John of Jerusalem. From that time our Lodges took the name of Lodges of St. John.

While Ramsay is generally regarded as the father of the Templar/ Mason connection he did not mention the earlier Order by name. It was actually the German, Baron Karl Von Hundt, who, perhaps drawing on Ramsay's earlier work, linked the Knights Templar to what would become the Masonic fraternity. Whether these connections were factual or simply the wishful thinking of past and present Freemasons, is unclear.

What we do know from historical records is that Freemasonry did develop Chivalric and Templar grades. In 1780, the Grand Lodge of York sanctioned the workings of five separate degrees: the Entered Apprentice, the Fellowcraft, the Master Mason, the Royal Arch, and the Knight Templar. At the time of union (1813) between the Antients and the Moderns (two rival Grand Lodges in England) the United Grand Lodge of England said the following:

It is declared and pronounced that pure Atient (sic) Masonry consists of three degrees, and no more viz: those of the entered apprentice, the Fellowcraft, and the Master Mason, including the Supreme Order of the Holy Royal Arch.

Most Freemasonic sources are quick to report this quotation as evidence that the higher degrees are not "higher degrees," and while this is on the surface true, it belies the fact that the United Grand Lodge of England, at the time of union, did support the Chivalric grades. The article goes on to say:

> This article is not intended to prevent any lodge or Chapter from holding meetings in any of the degrees of Chivalry, according to the Constitutions of said Order.

Prior to 1717, Freemasonry still maintained a strong undercurrent of Christianity in the symbolic structure of Craft Masonry, which was concurrent with all that Masonic Templarism was and is. When James Anderson wrote his constitutions of the craft in 1723, much of the Christian symbolism was removed in order that the fraternity might be more accessible to men of all faiths. Although this is an important and wonderful aspect of the Masonic fraternity, and one of the reasons Freemasonry has survived all these centuries, Christian Masons of the time sought out an order whereby they could continue the Christian symbolism that was inherent in the pre-Anderson fraternity. Such an order was the chivalric grades.

As indicated in an article from the United Grand Lodge of England, these chivalric degrees were in existence in 1813 and had been for some time, most likely evolving from the efforts of Chevalier Ramsay and Baron Von Hundt.

Templarism arrives in North America

Between 1710 and 1905, virtually every regiment of infantry and company of the Royal Artillery in the British Army was stationed (at some point), in Halifax and Quebec. In almost all cases there was an active Masonic Lodge within these regiments. One of these lodges, Lodge Glittering Star No. 33, as mentioned in Michael Kaulback's article, "The First

Knights Templar in the United States," received a warrant while in Ireland during the 1750s and 60s to confer the Knight Templar Order.

This lodge, along with lodges of the 14th and 59th Regiments, while in Halifax from 1763 to 1766, conferred the Order of the Temple, as well as the Royal Arch and Red Cross degrees. (It should be noted that there is no conclusive evidence that the Red Cross degree conferred at this time has any similarity to its present day form of Masonic Templarism.) In fact some sources indicate that it is closer to that conferred in today's "Red Cross of Constantine," an invitational Masonic body of the York Rite path of Freemasonry.

From Halifax, the three regiments were transferred to Boston, Massachusetts, where, in 1766 the order was conferred on brethren in the famed city of American independence (namely William Davis and Paul Revere). As this is covered in extensive detail in Kaulback's article, I will not comment on this more than to say that these conferrals are the earliest known records of the degrees and orders being issued on the North American continent.

At the time of the Boston initiations there were three active centers in Canada. These were in Montreal, Kingston, and Niagara.

In 1824, New Brunswick became a center of Canadian Masonic Templarism, and continued to be active until the year 1860. The Grand Priory of Scotland officially issued a warrant to the St. John Encampment in New Brunswick in 1856. For unknown reasons, a number of the members of this encampment broke away and formed the Union de Molay Encampment and Priory in 1869. They obtained a warrant from the Grand Conclave of England and Wales, which was the governing body at the time.

This schism caused a great deal of disharmony in Canadian Templarism, and this feeling continued from 1875 until 1915 (and included the temporary separation of fraternal relations between Canada, England, and Scotland). Additionally, the Scottish encampment in St. John united with the Sovereign Great Priory of Canada in 1897, but is on the records as existing from 1856, the date of its original Scottish warrant. But this is getting ahead of our story, for before the St. John Encampment could unite with the Sovereign Great Priory of Canada, this priory had to come into existence (and this involved a long and sometimes bitter battle).

Canada's first Grand Master

In 1852, Captain William James Bury McLeod Moore was transferred to Canada, where he was stationed at Kingston, Ontario. He soon set himself to the task of reviving the defunct Kingston Encampment, which had received its warrant nearly a quarter century earlier in 1824.

Approximately two years later, a warrant was issued by the Supreme Grand Conclave of England and Wales for Hugh de Payns Encampment. This Encampment is now known as "Hugh de Payns Premiere Preceptory," and is the oldest preceptory within the Sovereign Great Priory.

From the time of his arrival in Ontario, McLeod Moore was keen on forming a governing body for the purpose of supervising the activities of all encampments in the Province of Canada. In July of 1854, McLeod Moore received a

Canadian Templar Uniform, circa 1862. From private collection of Stephen Dafoe.

patent from the Supreme Grand Master of the Temple in England, granting him the rank of Provincial Grand Commander of the Order in the Province of Canada.

Within the next year there were three Encampments operating in the Province of Canada (the aforementioned Hugh de Payns in Kingston, Geoffrey de St. Aldemar in Toronto, and William de La More, the Martyr in Quebec). On October 9, 1855, the three encampments were called by the new Provincial Grand Commander to a meeting held at Kingston.

No representatives came from Geoffrey de St. Aldemar, which was likely due to the difficulties traveling between Toronto and Kingston (a three-hour drive by today's standards, certainly a much longer journey by horse). In all, 13 Templars attended this first Provincial Grand Conclave for the Province of Canada. It was directed by the Supreme Grand Conclave in England that Hugh de Payns Encampment in Kingston would hold rank in the body, and that their rank would be effective from February 12, 1824—the date of their original warrant.

The jewels of Hugh de Payns Encampment were loaned to the Provincial Grand Conclave until such time as others could be procured for the new body.

Although Canada, at this time, was hardly a coast to coast concern, this initial Grand Provincial Conclave was the precursor of what is today known as The Sovereign Great Priory of Canada. Today that governing body covers the country from its easternmost to westernmost coasts.

A mere nine days after the Grand Provincial Conclave, the Grand Encampment of Ireland issued a warrant to the Templars of Hamilton, Ontario. This encampment then joined the Provincial Grand Conclave in 1859 as the "Godfrey de Bouillon Encampment."

Fraternal relations between Canadian and American Templars were formed quickly, with the General Grand Master of the United States officially recognizing the Canadian "Fratres" at the Second Annual Assembly, held in Kingston in 1856. It was at this assembly that the rules and regulations for the governance of the Provincial Grand Conclave were adopted. The two offices that were to be filled by election were those of the Grand Treasurer and the Grand Equerry. (Although the term Equerry is defined as "a person in charge of the horses of princes and nobles," the office most certainly was charged with the general affairs and properties of the order—similar to a modern Grand Secretary.) The Provincial Grand Commander, William McLeod Moore, appointed all of the remaining officers to their positions.

During the next decade, Canadian encampments continued to grow in number. By 1867, the year of the Canadian Confederation, there were eight encampments. These were Hugh de Payns (in Kingston), William de La More (in Ottawa)—which had moved from its former home of Quebec, Richard de Coeur de Lion (in London), Godfrey de Bouillon (in Hamilton), King Baldwin (in Belleville), Richard de Coeur de Lion (in Montreal), Plantagenet (in St. Catherines), and Sussex (in Stanstead). Absent from the roster was Geoffrey de St. Aldemar, of Toronto. This encampment, which had lost all of its property and equipment in a fire, had become dormant. It was later revived in 1870.

One of the interesting additions to the roster of encampments at the 1867 assembly was the Godfrey de Bouillon, which had received its warrant from Ireland in 1855. Until the Godfrey de Bouillon Encampment joined the Provincial Grand Conclave in 1859, Canadian Templarism did not confer the Order of Malta. With the transfer of this encampment to the Conclave, the Grand Commander, McLeod Moore, authorized all

Canadian encampments to confer the order and it has remained a major part of Canadian Templarism to this day (being the second of the Chivalric Orders conferred in our Preceptories). With the addition of this then-honorary order, the Grand Commander added to his titles, "Grand Commander Masonic Knights of Malta."

At the 1867 meeting, which was the 12th Annual Assembly of the Provincial Grand Conclave, two important recommendations were made:

1. The Provincial Grand Conclave apply to the Supreme Grand Conclave of England for the appointment of a Colonial Deputy Grand Master for the Dominion of Canada, with power to establish Provincial Grand Conclaves in the Provinces of the Dominion.

2. The correspondences be originated with the Supreme Grand body in England to express the desire to form a Supreme Grand Conclave for the Dominion of Canada, with Colonel W. J. B. McLeod Moore as its first Grand Master.

In answer to the Colonials request, W. J. B. McLeod Moore was appointed Grand Prior on May 18, 1868. In this capacity he was head of the Grand Priory of the Dominion of Canada, and was under the jurisdiction of the Supreme Grand Conclave of England and Wales. (Excluded from his jurisdiction was the Nova Scotia Encampment No. 58 in Halifax, the Union de Molay Encampment No. 104 in St. John, New Brunswick, and the St. John Encampment No. 48—the latter of which was still under Scottish jurisdiction.)

The Grand Priory of the Dominion of Canada held its first assembly on August 12, 1868 in Montreal. There were 25 Sir Knights in attendance. McLeod Moore, as Grand Prior, held absolute authority. In his

Grand Historian's report of 1984, Reg. Forest-Jones recounts an incident where the members of the order expressed a desire to change the uniform of the order and adapt garments similar to that of their American Brethren (in order to be able to take part in Masonic procession). Forest-Jones quotes the words of McLeod Moore as follows:

> For my part, I cannot agree with the necessity for this change. The Order of the Temple as now constituted, was never intended for public gaze or street display, and the modern innovations of a military uniform and drill, so much though of in the United States, do not convey to my mind the dignified position we ought to assume as successors—although by adoption—of our predecessors, the knights of old…I am strongly opposed to all public displays and deprecate them most strenuously…there is too great a desire to blazon forth all our doings, which can neither be understood or appreciated by the public at large….If the opportunity of exhibiting themselves in public with an attractive costume can really be the principal inducement for persons wishing to join the Order, such accessions to our rank would do us but little credit.

It is interesting to note that at some future point (although I have yet to find the exact date) the uniform did change, and Canadian Templars adopted a style similar to their American counterparts. Gone was the pillbox-style chapeau, which was replaced with a Navy style plumed hat. This hat was in existence as early as 1940, but was replaced in 1962 with the current pillbox chapeau of red felt. This change in haberdashery was not the first time that the Order would get back to the basics.

Back to the basics

By the early 1870s, a movement was arising in the United Kingdom. A body calling itself the Convent General had formed as the result of negotiations between England, Wales, Ireland, and Scotland. The purpose of the body was to regulate the matters of the Order in these countries. The resulting body was to be known as The United Religious and Military Order of the Temple and of St. John of Jerusalem, Palestine, Rhodes, and Malta.

While England, Wales, and Ireland were in agreement, at the last moment, Scotland opted not to sign. The Royal Highness, the Prince of Wales, was to be the head of the new body and Queen Victoria was the Grand Patron of the Order. The true purpose of the new body was to restore the Order of the Temple, in so far as possible, to its original ancient statutes and constitutions. Among these changes was a desire to revert to the original ceremonies and rituals. This included a reversion to the original nomenclatures. Thus "Grand Conclaves" became "Great Priories," and "encampments" became "preceptories." No longer were the heads of the preceptories referred to by the rank of Commander; they were now given the rank and title of Preceptor. The Prelates became Chaplains and the former first and second Captains were called Constable and Marshal respectively. The Governing body would be known as the Convent General, and at this point in time the use of the word Masonic was discontinued from Templarism. No longer did the Order confer the Honorary "Past Rank," but instead a new Order was instituted, which would confer the Chivalric ranks of Knight Grand Cross (G.C.T.) and Knight Commander of the Temple (K.C.T.). This new honor was restricted in its number of members and was conferred on Preceptors alone.

It comes as no surprise that the honor of G.C.T. was first conferred on Colonel Moore, who had served as Grand Prior since 1855, and would continue in the office until 1889. The honor was also conferred on John Quincy Adams, Grand Master of the General Grand Encampment of the United States, along with 25 others (among them the King of Sweden and the Emperor of Germany).

As Canadian Templarism began to take form and adopt the titles and ranks that were familiar to modern day members of the Order in Canada, resolutions were passed that outlined the requirements for membership as follows:

- Prospective candidates were required to be at least 21 years old (a requirement traditional in Freemasonry, and in keeping with the original requirements of the Order in the Crusader era).

- A candidate needed to be a Royal Arch Mason and a Master Mason for at least two years standing.

- The candidate must be a professor of the doctrine of the Holy and Undivided Trinity. (An interesting side note is that this requirement remained unchanged for 130 years, until 2001/ 2002, when Supreme Grand Master, Larry J. Hostine, changed the ruling to read "profess the doctrine of the Holy and Undivided Christian Trinity." In the late 1800s and early 1900s there could be no doubt as to the interpretation of the Trinity. However modern times have caused some to seek admission in the Order who were not of the Christian faith, but did follow a religious path that included a Trinity. This change was made to avoid any confusion.

- Additionally, the candidate of the 1800s needed to be willing to accept the statutes and ordinances of the Order—present and future. His ballot must be unanimous. (This regulation was changed in 1903, and a ballot could contain three black balls before a candidate was rejected.)

- The admission fee for a prospective candidate was to be not less than 5 guineas (about $43 in today's currency). Interestingly, the admission fee in Canada is presently $125.00 plus the current year's dues.

The changes by the General Convent in the United Kingdom led the Canadian Templars to take steps towards a more autonomous existence. A communication was sent to the Grand Master in the United Kingdom which expressed a desire for Canadian Templars to have more self-governance.

Unfortunately, in this letter no mention was made regarding the Provincial Grand Conclaves of Nova Scotia and New Brunswick. Additionally, the document did not have the cooperation of Quebec, and the eastern provinces were not solicited for their opinions on the matter. The oversight did not go unnoticed in England—Moore's petition was rejected.

But good fortune later fell on Moore. Soon after his petition (in December of 1873), the Honorable Alexander Keith, Provincial Grand Prior of Nova Scotia, died. Keith was a prominent Canadian, a former mayor of Halifax, director of the bank of Nova Scotia and president of the upper house of the Nova Scotia legislature. (Sadly, he is best known today in Canada for the beer that carries his name.) With the death of Keith, the powers that be in the United Kingdom informed Moore that the whole of Canada would now be under his jurisdiction.

With the control he had desired for Canadian Templarism in his hands, there were still preceptories outside his governance (these were the Scottish warranted preceptories at St. Stephen and St. John New Brunswick, as well as an Irish-warranted preceptory in Hawkesbury Ontario).

Although Moore was the effective head of Canadian Templarism, autonomy was slow in coming. On July 28, 1876 a patent was issued that admitted Canada to the Convent General. Canadian Templars were placed under the jurisdiction of The National Great Priory of Canada, which in turn was under the guidance of the convent General.

For reasons unknown there was some dissension among the ranks, and in the fall of 1876 a good number of the Templars in Ontario tried to establish an independent Grand Commandery (in alliance with the Grand Encampment of the United States). Fortunately, for Canadian Templarism, this movement died out, and today all Canadian Masonic preceptories are under the banner of the Sovereign Great Priory of Canada.

Meanwhile, all was not well with the National Great Priory of Canada. Apparently, they were not altogether pleased with their new membership in the Convent General. Moore felt that each Great Priory should be permitted to frame its own regulations, titles, ranks, and rituals. As a result of the control of the Convent General, by 1880 wherever the words "Convent General" appeared in the Canadian statutes, they were deleted. This was in essence a "declaration of independence" by the National Great Priory of Canada.

In 1883, at the Annual assembly an address was sent to the Prince of Wales (later known as King Edward VII), the Supreme Grand Master of the United Kingdom. This address absolved the National Great Priory of Canada from any allegiance to him and, in so doing, established itself as an independent Great Priory.

Moore was unanimously elected Great Prior of Canada for life. Soon after, the official absolution was received from the United Kingdom, along with well wishes for the Great Priory of Canada and all its members. Moore, upon receiving the absolution, immediately made a proclamation that all preceptories of the Order of the Temple and Knights of Malta were under his authority, and that their allegiance was to him and the National Great Priory of Canada alone.

In 1884, at what would be the final assembly of the National Great Priory of Canada, necessary resolutions were passed to change the name of the governing body to that of The Sovereign Great Priory of Canada. Moore was elected as Supreme Grand Master for life. The other officers of the new Sovereign Great Priory were elected to their positions and invested by Sir Knight Theodore S. Parvin, who was then Grand Secretary of the Grand Encampment of the United States.

At the time of its formation, the Sovereign Great Priory of Canada consisted of 26 preceptories. The majority of these (20 in all) were in Ontario. Another three were in Quebec, and the provinces of Nova Scotia, New Brunswick, and Manitoba each had one. In total, these 26 preceptories contained 795 Templars.

Moore continued as Grand Master of Canadian Templars until his death on September 1, 1890. His funeral was held in Prescott, Ontario, and he was buried in Mount Royal Cemetery in Montreal, Quebec. As an interesting side note, each year Templars from across the country gather at the resting place of the first Grand Master; a public procession of which Moore probably would not have approved.

Moore was succeeded by the Deputy Grand Master, Most Eminent Knight James Alexander Henderson, who was invested and installed as Canada's second Supreme Grand Master on November 17, 1890. In addition to holding the distinction of being Canada's second Grand Master, and one of the first candidates for Templarism initiated in Hugh de Payns Premiere Preceptory, Henderson is also Canada's shortest-lived Grand Master. Henderson died after only 20 days in office. It is ironic that the first and second Grand Masters of Canadian Templarism would serve the longest and shortest terms of office respectively.

In all there have been 62 Supreme Grand Masters of the Sovereign Great Priory of Canada. After the death of Henderson, the term of office for the Grand Master was designated a period of one year. Just three years later, in 1893 it was resolved that the term of office would be for a period of two years. It continues to be the case up to the present time.

Today, Canada's Masonic Knights Templar gather at 77 preceptories, broken down into 15 districts, across the country. There has not been a new preceptory started in Canada since 1986, when Kamloops Preceptory Number 84, in Kamloops, British Columbia, received its warrant for the Sovereign Great Priory.

In 2002, Cornwall Preceptory No. 47 turned in its charter and ceased to exist. (It had been active since it was warranted on August 14, 1907, and this ending nearly a century of Templarism in Eastern Ontario. The demise of Cornwall Preceptory No. 47 was due, in large part, to a decline in membership—and a decline in the attendance of those who still held membership. In 2000, the last year for which I have statistics, the Preceptory had 56 members, a decline of nearly 10 percent from the previous year.)

The now defunct Cornwall Preceptory did not stand alone in its loss of members. Similar to many branches of Freemasonry and other organizations for that matter, the membership of Canadian Templarism is aging. With each passing year, more members pass away than seek admission into this great Masonic Order. In the Annual Proceedings of 2001, it was recorded that in 1999 there were 11,310 members of the Order in Canada. While this is a far greater number than the 795 members in 1884, a further study of the statistics shows that membership is definitely on the decline. In 1999 there were 209 new members who joined the ranks of the Order. Another 17 affiliated from other areas, and 35 members, who had previously left the order, rejoined their Masonic-Templar fellowships. By comparison, 372 of our members passed away. Another 474 left the Order, and 290 were suspended (mostly for nonpayment of dues). This left a net loss in membership of 875 members. At this rate of attrition, it could easily be predicted that the Order is in trouble, and certainly on the decline.

It is quite possible that the decision of "The Ancient Arabic Order of the Nobles of the Mystic Shrine," better known as The Shriners, to change their membership requirements in 2000 may have a further short-term effect on Masonic Templarism in Canada. (Until July 3, 2000, candidates for membership were required to be either Knights Templar or Scottish Rite Masons.) With the removal of this requirement, Royal Arch Chapters and preceptories have seen an increase in the number of withdrawals from the Order.

Although this is problematic in the short term, I believe it will not be a long-lasting effect. For the past 124 years the Royal Arch and the Masonic Knights Templar have relied on the Shriners to be somewhat of a recruiting tool for membership. Many of those who joined the Order did so as a stepping stone to the Shrine. With this requirement removed from the equation, those who are now petitioning to be Masonic Knights Templar are doing so out of a pure desire to be a Templar Mason. In this sense, we are now creating a new generation of Chivalric Masons who are as dedicated to Canadian Masonic Templarism as those men who helped Moore build the order in this country in the middle years of the 19th century.

The Early History of Freemasonry
By Robert Lomas

The earliest documentary evidence for the existence of Freemasonic rituals is to be found on the south wall of a small, 15th century Church in Mid-Lothian, Scotland, now known as Rosslyn Chapel. It was built between 1441 and 1486 by William St. Clair (who was Earl of Caithness, third and last St. Clair Earl of Orkney, Baron of Roslin, and Lord Sinclair). As Chancellor and High Admiral of Scotland, Sinclair was the second most powerful man in the kingdom. Indeed, he seems to have even threatened the power of the Stuart kings.

At the time when James II was getting deeply embroiled in English politics, William started to build what was then known as Roslin chapel. When James II was killed during the War of the Roses (at the Battle of Roxbourgh), his son James III stripped William of the earldom of Orkney and forced him to split his land between his many children. The St. Clairs' power was thus broken, and they were never again strong enough to challenge the Stuart's grip on the crown of Scotland.

I will consider the St. Clairs of Roslin a bit further, but first let me explain how Freemasonic rituals can be shown to have existed in the time of William St. Clair, the builder of Roslin Chapel.

The new chapel William was building at Roslin was a tremendously ambitious project. The entire surface of the building, inside and out, was to be carved with tremendously ornate detail. Father Hay, the historian of Roslin, tells us that William personally supervised all the decoration, insisting that every piece was first carved in wood and presented for his inspection before he allowed them to be carved into the stone.

If Father Hay is correct, then William St. Clair was the first exponent of quality control in his building works. More importantly perhaps, the implication of this statement is that none of the strange tableaus carved into the structure are there by either accident, or by the whim of individual Masons with a sense of humour. The fox, wearing clergyman's robes, standing in a pulpit lecturing to a congregation of chickens, tells us something about William's opinions of the priests of the Church.

But it is a small tableaux in the external southeastern corner that is the earliest evidence of what is today known as speculative Freemasonry. The scene shows a man kneeling in a very strange posture—his feet are placed in the form of a square, in his left hand he holds a bible, he is blindfolded, and has a running noose about his neck. Alongside him stands a bearded man, robed as a Knight Templar, who holds the noose. This strange pair are placed between two pillars. With the exception of the medieval clothing of the kneeling man, this scene could be a depiction of a modern Masonic first degree ceremony.

Once I had realized how many similarities there are between this carving and a modern Freemasonic ceremony, I began to comment on this during my lectures, and eventually published the evidence in a book coauthored with Christopher Knight, *The Second Messiah*. On many occasions, I have been asked to debate this evidence within Masonic lodges, and on American and British radio.

During these debates the librarian of the Grand Lodge, in London, suggested that my conclusions that this was evidence of Masonic ritual in use in Scotland in the mid 15th century could be explained away as simple coincidence.

However, one of the subjects I happen to teach is Statistics. And in one of my regular lectures I look at the wider scope of statistical analysis, in hopes of determining the importance of evidence. So, as a demonstration, I decided to undertake a careful analysis of the suggestion that the similarities between William St. Clair's authorized carving and the modern first degree of Freemasonry were pure chance.

My results were conclusive. Even if I gave the highest possible probability to things happening by chance, there is only a probability of two parts in a thousand that all the similar elements to the modern first degree are there by pure accident. To a statistician, the facts are that William did not mix all these disparate elements by accident, unless he was incredibly lucky. He probably meant to have all those factors together when he approved the piece. The same "landmarks" survive into modern Freemasonry, which claims to have preserved them from "our ancient brethren."

This piece of evidence disproves the hypothesis that the elements of Freemasonic rituals included in the tableaux could have been included by pure chance (as the Librarian of the United Grand Lodge of England, who is not a statistician, had suggested). It leaves intact the alternative hypothesis I had put forward, that the ceremony was known to the builder of Roslin Chapel in the mid 15th century.

The next piece of evidence linking Masons to a ritual connected with Solomon's Temple was noticed by historian David Stevenson, of St. Andrews University. (Stevenson is not a Mason.) The evidence comes from "Aberdeen." In the west front of King's College, Aberdeen is the Latin inscription that Stevenson translates as:

> By the grace of the most serene, illustrious and ever-
> victorious King James IV: On the fourth before the nones
> of April in the year one-thousand five-hundred the Masons
> began to build this excellent college.

Stevenson goes on to point in his book, *The Origins of Freemasonry*, that the date is significant for Freemasons, as it is the date traditionally accepted for the commencement of the construction of Solomon's Temple.

Stevenson goes on to comment further, saying:

> This, however, does not explain the peculiar wording of the inscription. It mentions the king as patron of the project but states that 2 April was the date on which the masons started work. It is surprising that an inscription of this sort should specifically mention the craftsmen responsible for the work at all and yet here they are standing alongside the king.

(James IV married Margaret Tudor, the eldest daughter of Henry VII of England, an act which eventually led to James VI of Scotland becoming king of England.)

As Stevenson explains:

> By the late sixteenth century the Craft was in fact on the verge of a remarkable development which would make it different...one man saw that some aspects of the traditional heritage of the craft of masonry linked up a whole series of trends in the thought and culture of the age, and worked to introduce them in the craft.

That man was William Schaw, who, on December 21, 1583, became Master of Works to King James VI and Queen Anne.

William Schaw, the great architect of the craft

William Schaw was born around 1550 in Clackmannan, near Stirling. His father, John Schaw of Broich, had been keeper of the king's wine cellar. By the age of 10 years, William was employed at court as a page to

Mary of Guise (we know this because the Queen Dowager's accounts recorded his name on the list of her retainers for whom mourning was purchased). That same year, his father John was charged with murdering the servant of another Laird.

William next appeared in Scottish records when he signed the "Negative Confession," a document that James VI and his courtiers had to swear by in order to assure the Reformed Church that the king and his retinue were not trying to bring back the Catholic Faith. (William was a Catholic, but seems to have been flexible enough in his religious attitudes to stay out of trouble with the Kirk. As Stevenson comments: "Like a number of other Scots in court circles, though remaining a Catholic he avoided actions that might provoke persecution, probably attending Protestant services from time to time."

Schaw became James VI's Master of Works towards the end of 1583. About a month after his appointment, the king sent him on diplomatic mission to France (on the basis of his diplomatic, as well as building, skills). This seems to be confirmed by the fact that the king chose Schaw to help entertain the ambassadors of the king of Denmark, who came to negotiate the restoration of Orkney and Shetland to Denmark.

Schaw must have got on well with the Danes, because in 1589 James sent him back to Denmark to escort his new bride, Anne of Denmark, to Scotland. Schaw went on to become Queen Anne's Chamberlain, and a great favorite of hers. As his monument recalls:

> Queen Anne ordered a monument to be set up to the memory of a most admirable and most upright man lest the recollection of his high character, which deserves to be honoured for all time, should fade as his body cumbles into dust.

It was in 1590 that Schaw began to take an interest in Masons and their organization. The first written evidence of this is a letter composed under the authority of the king's Privy Seal, and addressed to Patrick Copland of Udoch (near Aberdeen) confirming his right to act as "wardanie over the maister masons of Aberdene, Banff, and Kincarne." Stevenson believes that Schaw may have been considering reorganizing the mason Craft under a number of regional wardens, and therefore used the historical precedent of the Coplands of Udoch to reestablished the principle of regional wardens. However, eight years after confirming the authority of a regional warden in Aberdeenshire by privy seal, Schaw took on himself the role of general warden of the Craft of Scotland. The post was a new one that Schaw created, and it met with the approval of a number of unnamed "maister maissounis," who attended a meeting on the Feast of St. John (in Edinburgh) in 1598.

Schaw, who was the king's Master of Works, acted as agent for the throne in all state building works. This gave him a great deal of control over the Masons of Scotland, and so he was only rationalizing a state of affairs that was already in existence. His first Statues contained 22 clauses.

The first clause insists that all Masons "observe and keep all the good ordinances set down before, concerning the privileges of their Craft set down by their predecessors of good memory and that they be true to one another and live charitably together as becomes sworn brethren and companions of the Craft." Here Schaw is referring to a system of regulations still known to Masons as the Antient Charges.

The remaining clauses deal with how the lodges shall be ruled and governed, and how the work of the masons should be managed. There are two particularly interesting items. One contains the first health and safety directive ever issued within the building trade. It says: "That all masiteris, in charge of works, be very careful to see their scaffolds and ladders are surely set and placed, to the effect that through their negligence and sloth no hurt or harm come unto any persons that works at the said work, under pain of discharging of them hereafter from working as masiteris having charge of any work, but they shall be subject all the rest of their days to work under or with another principle masiter having charge of the work." Stern discipline indeed, for any Master Mason who did not take care that his workers were properly secured when they worked in the dizzy heights of a great cathedral or a Scottish grand house. Today's factory inspectorate would not quarrel with the intentions and sanctions of this 16th-century Masonic legislation.

The other interesting item concerns how the Master of a Lodge shall be chosen: "That there be a warden chosen and elected each year to have the charge over every lodge…to the effect that the General Warden may send such directions to that elected warden as required."

The Master of the Lodge [Warden] has to be elected each year, and Schaw, as General Warden of the Craft intended to issue any instructions via the elected officers of the Lodge to the Masons. This was a highly-democratic system he put in place (some 50 years before the Civil War got around to addressing the same questions of democratic accountability in England).

All in all, this was a far-sighted and fair document, and it has the obvious intention of simplifying the general management of Masons in Scotland. It takes account of the ancient traditions of the order and respects existing rituals, makes proper provision for safe working practices, and provides for regular democratic feedback from the "Maisteris" of the Lodge. It was issued with the endorsement of all the Master Masons who had attended the Feast of St. John meeting in Edinburgh in 1598, as the closing sentences show: "And for fulfiling and observing of these ordinance, set down as said here, the group of maisteris here assembled this day binds and obligies themselves hereto to be faithful. And therefore has requested the said General Warden to sign them with his own hand, to the effect that an authentic copy hereof may be sent to every particular lodge within this realm."

This document is also the first time that any lodge has been instructed to keep written records of its proceedings. (The oldest lodge minutes in existence are those of Edinburgh's St. Mary's Chapel, which started immediately after this meeting with Schaw.)

The first Schaw statute tells us a lot about early Freemasonry. It demonstrates that our antient Scottish brethren met in lodges, that these lodges were ruled by Masters or Wardens, that there was a system of meetings at a higher level than the lodge, that lodges were obliged to keep written records of their activities, and that they were bound to observe the antient ordinances of their craft. All of these aspects have survived within modern Freemasonry, and this is the earliest written evidence of their introduction.

Schaw formalized the present-day system of Masonic lodges. A lodge is not just the building where Masons meet—it is also the body of men who make up that group. It has its own traditions, hierarchy, and records to prove what it has decided—but it is basically a democratic unit inherited from a time when democracy was not yet supposed to have been invented.

However, there is more to this story, because a well-established lodge existed out on the west coast of Scotland. This lodge, known today as Mother Kilwinning, was not based in Edinburgh, but rather on the coast of Ayr, on the grounds of Kilwinning Abbey. The Wardens of Mother Kilwinning Lodge were accustomed to issuing charters to other groups of masons—so that these groups could form themselves into new lodges—and they claimed rights over the Mason Craft in Aryshire.

Schaw's first Statue did not recognize the rule that Kilwinning claimed in the newly-created Masonic ranking. The following year, 1599, on the Feast of St. John, Schaw issued his second statue, this time from Holyrood House (one of the king's palaces). They confirmed the statements in the first statue, but went on to assign a formal status to Kilwinning Lodge.

When Schaw had held his first formal meeting as General Warden of the Craft, again on the Feast Day of St. John the Evangelist, Kilwinning Lodge sent Brother Archebald Barclay to present a case that it should have a role in the new way of ruling the craft. Barclay was successful in making his case, as Schaw went on to confirm that Kilwinning should be allowed to maintain its ancient practice of electing its officers on the eve of the winter solstice. It was also assigned the rank of "second lurge of Scotland," and its wardens were to have the right to be present at the election of all other Wardens of Lodges within Lanarkshire, Glasgow, Ayr, and Carrick. A Warden of Kilwinning was to have the power to summon and judge all wardens of lodges within this area, with power delegated by Schaw as General Warden of the Craft. The Wardens of Kilwinning were to conduct regular tests of the Masons within their jurisdiction to ensure they were properly trained in "the art and craft of science and of memory."

With this clarification of the most important of the ancient ordinances, and the adjustment to the pecking order between St Mary's Chapel and Kilwinning, Schaw apparently had settled Freemasonry into a more stable structure. However, he had even greater ambitions for his fledging new organization. Schaw wanted the king to become Grand Master of the Order, and he wanted a Royal Charter to confirm this status on the Craft for ever.

He had one problem. The Masons would not accept a cowan as their Grand Master. Even though he was king, if James was to become the Grand Master Mason, he would first have to become a Mason.

In 1584, Schaw had assisted his close friend Alexander Seton (later Earl of Dunfermline, and a member of Aberdeen Lodge) in designing a house for Lord Somerville. The master mason employed to carry out the work was John Mylne. In 1601 Mylne was Master of the Lodge of Scoon and Perth. This lodge was situated in Scoon, (modern spelling, Scone) which is the ancient place of the coronation of the Kings of Scotland. (The kings of Scots have traditionally been crowned at Moot Hill, within the grounds of the palace of Scoon. So, Scoon was a fitting place for a king to be made a Mason.)

Brother, his majesty King James VI

On the wall of the Lodge of Scoon and Perth hangs a painting of a very important Masonic event (the initiation of King James VI). The official entry of the Lodge on the Roll of the Grand Lodge of Scotland simply says the lodge existed before 1658. This date refers to the charter of the Lodge, and is a set of rules that explain how the lodge was governed. The document is signed by the Right Worshipful Master (J. Roch), and two wardens (Mr. Measone and Mr. Norie). This same charter records the event depicted on the wall of the lodge room. The Charter states: "In the reigne of his Majesty King James the sixth, of blessed Memorie, who, by the said John John Mylne was by the king's own desire entered Freeman, meason and Fellow-Craft. During his lifetime he mantayned the same as ane member of the Lodge of Scoon, so that this lodge is the most famous lodge within the kingdom."

As I have mentioned, the Mylne family figure a great deal in the early history of Freemasonry—no less than three generations of them (all with the Christian name of John) held the Mastership of the Lodge of Scoon and Perth between the late 1500s and 1658, when the Scoon Charter says the mastership passed to James Roch. This James Roch was the signatory to the document that records the making of James VI as a Freemason in 1601.

The second John Mylne (son of the John who initiated King James) had carved a statue of the king in Edinburgh in 1616. In 1631, this Mylne was appointed Master Mason to Charles I, and in 1636 resigned the office in favor of his eldest son, also named John Mylne (all the Mylnes seemed to call their eldest sons John), who had been made a Fellow Craft of the Lodge of Edinburgh in 1633. This third John Mylne took part in Masonic meeting in Newcastle in 1641, where Sir Robert Moray was made a Mason (Moray is the first Mason documented as having been made on English soil).

So, the grandson of the man who initiated James VI went on to initiate Moray. There is every reason to believe that Moray received a family account of the initiation of James VI, and may have been well aware of the close links between the Stuart kings and Freemasonry before he became involved with them. Moray went on to found the Royal Society, which is still one of the most important scientific societies in the world today.

But the real question that needs to be asked is how James VI, King of Scots, came to be made a member of a lodge of Freemasons?

The political purpose of the king being made a Mason should now be clear. To complete his designs for the craft, Schaw needed the king to be a Mason. James VI loved ritual, masques, and dressing up. From all accounts he would have delighted in the initiation ceremony. Schaw now had every thing he needed in place to propose a Royal Grand Master

Mason for the craft, to be followed with the issue of the Royal Charter that confirmed his authority as Lord General Warden of the Craft. However, the Masons of Scotland had different ideas.

The Scots claimed a different Grand Master (William Sinclair, Laird of Roslin, and the direct descendant of the man who had carved the statue of the candidates in 1440).

William the Wastrel

When Schaw had created his second statue, he had been on the verge of obtaining a Royal sanction for the privileges of the craft. However, at this point it appears he was forced into backtracking. A powerful group of Masons insisted that he issue a document, now known as the First St. Clair Charter. Of this document, Stevenson writes:

> [It] can be seen as indicating...that Schaw was forced to change his plans [for obtaining a Royal Charter] to take account of claims of the Craft...which were too strong for him to resist...Schaw's death in 1602 and the move of the king to England on the union of the Crowns the following year may have disrupted sttempts to win the king's support.

Now that Schaw had confirmed the claims of Kilwinning in its role as a minor Grand Lodge, the other lodges had recognized that Schaw could be put under pressure, and could be made to adjust his ideas. Obtaining the agreement of the Lodge of Scoon and Perth to initiate King James VI seemed to have been Schaw's first move towards uniting the Lodges of Scotland under the Grand Mastership of the king. (There is a Masonic Order which automatically makes the reigning King of Scots its Grand Master, known as the Royal Order of Scotland.) The consequence of James's making the Lodge of Scoon and Perth his mother Lodge would, as the minutes say, be "so that this lodge is the most famous lodge within the kingdom."

This move would undermine all the jockeying for position which had gone on earlier. Edinburgh had already been named as first lodge, Kilwinning was officially number two, and Stirling was positioned third in seniority. But now, as the Royal Grand Master's Lodge, Scoon and Perth was poised to take precedence over all other lodges. By initiating the king, the Lodge of Scoon and Perth was outflanking all of their brother Masons.

Schaw was now put under pressure by the Lodges in the east of Scotland (Edinburgh, St. Andrews, Haddington, Achieson, Haven, and Dunfermlin) to acknowledge another ancient authority in Freemasonry, that of William St. Clair of Roslin. As Stevenson comments: "Though in William Sinclair the masons has found a gentleman of ancient lineage willing to be their patron, they had not found a respectable or influential one....If the masons had had a free choice in seeking a suitable patron to advance the craft's interests they would never had chosen the laird of Roslin!"

William St. Clair, third and last St. Clair Earl of Orkney, and the builder of Rosslyn Chapel (where the oldest evidence of Masonic ritual is carved into the wall) had been the second most powerful man in Scotland until 1471, when he had been forced to split up his holdings. The Baronies of Roslin and Pentland had been transferred to one of his son's (Oliver, Lord Sinclair). From Oliver they had then passed first to another William, and then to an Edward, before vesting in the particular William Sinclair we are concerned with.

This William Sinclair was a Catholic who kept falling foul of the Kirk. He used Rosslyn Chapel to have one of his children baptised in 1589.

(Rosslyn was not a Parish church, but William was unperturbed by the outcry this caused.) The minister who conducted the service, however, was forced make a public plea for forgiveness. A year later, the presbytery of Dalkeith accused Sinclair of "keiping images and uther monuments of idolatrie" in Rosslyn.

The Kirk officials had to postpone interviewing him, however, as he had been arrested and charged with threatening the king's person. When he was freed, the Kirk pursued him, insisting that Rosslyn should not be used as a place of worship and insisting that William force his tenants to attend the parish Kirk. They also suggested he set an example and become an elder of the Kirk. William declined, saying he was "insufficient" for the position. He proved his point soon afterward, when he was forced to make a public confession of fornication with local a barmaid.

To add insult to injury, he told the Kirk he could not remember if all of his bastards had been baptized. When he was ordered to do public penance for his acts of fornication (by sitting on the repentance stool), he refused unless he was he was supplied with a quart of good wine to help him pass the time.

If one were to judge from the number of summons issued to Sinclair to keep the peace and to refrain from attacking individuals, it would seem that he was fond of both wenching and brawling.

Hay, the historian of the Sinclair family, described him as "a lewd man, who kept a millar's daughter for the purpose of fornication." He eventually ran away to Ireland with his mistress, abandoning his wife, his son William (there are a lot of William Sinclairs in this story!), and the Craft of Scotland.

This, then, was the man the Masons of Scotland preferred to have as their Patron, rather than let the Lodge of Scoon and Perth take precedence over them. William the Wastrel, as the Laird of Roslin was the known, had his power as the last St. Clair Earl of Orkney behind his claim, and he was the keeper of the most important Freemasonic shrine in Scotland, Rosslyn Chapel. His patronage was the only way to thwart the ambitions of the Mylne family (which Schaw had unleashed, via the Lodge Scoon and Perth). The claim of the Laird of Roslin could be supported by appealing to the first sentence of the first Schaw statue: "…that they observe and keep all the good ordinances set down before concerning the privileges of their Craft by their predecessors of good memory."

The First St. Clair Charter takes just this line when it says:

> Be it known to all man that the Deacons, Maistres and Freeman of the Masons with the realm of Scotland with the express consent and assent of William Schaw, Maister of Work to our Sovereign Lord do assert that from age to age it has been observed amongst us that the Lairds of Rosling has ever been Patrons and Protectors of use and our privileges like as our predecessors has obeyed and acknowledged them as Patrons and Protectors.

So, it would seem that Schaw's attempt to obtain a Royal Charter for the Freemasons failed because some lodges insisted on adhering to an older tradition (which linked them to the Sinclairs of Roslin). The outrageous character of the man they gave their loyalty to suggests that the tradition must have been important to them. Otherwise they could have gone along with Schaw's plan and taken James VI as their new Royal Patron. Certainly, the king's joining of the Craft had encouraged many of his courtiers to also join the Masons. Among them Lord Alexander, Lord Hamilton, and David Ramsey (Clockmaker to the king and gentleman of the Privy Chamber) who joined the Lodge of Edinburgh.

When James moved to London he continued to take part in ceremonies that involved acting out the role of King Solomon (the role taken by the master of the Lodge during the opening and closing ceremonies). And he certainly does not seem to have been secretive about it. Sir John Harrington, who spent an evening at James VI's court while he was entertaining King Christian of Denmark in 1617, reports: "After dinner the ladies and gentlemen of the Court enacted the Queen of Sheba coming to King Solomon's Temple. The lady who took the part of the Queen of Sheba was, however, too drunk to keep her balance on the steps and fell over onto King Christian's lap, covering him with wine, cream, jelly, beverages, cakes, spices, and other good matters that she was carrying in her hands.

This was not the only occasion James was reported to have carried out dramas connected with Solomon's Temple. James, however, became so obsessed with reenacting the story of the events surrounding Solomon's Temple that his courtiers dubbed him the British Solomon. But he also carried out regular Freemasonic ceremonies. As William Preston reports: "In 1607, the foundation stone of this elegant structure [part of the Palace of Whitehall] was laid by king James, and his wardens who were attended by many brothers, clothed in form. The ceremony was conducted with the greatest pomp and splendor."

So, prior to his coming to England, James VI, through his Master of Works William Schaw, developed the modern lodge system of Freemasonry in Scotland. By the time James had been initiated into Freemasonry at the Lodge of Scoon and Perth in 1601, he had become fascinated with the rituals of Solomon's Temple (which form an important part of the basis of Freemasonry). James had made Speculative Masonry fashionable in his court in Scotland, and then brought the rituals of Freemasonry to England.

Bibliography

Chapter 1: The Historical Beginnings of a Knightly Order

A Brief History of the Knights Templar

William of Tyre. *A History of Deeds beyond the Sea*. Trans, Emily Atwater Babcock and A.C. Krey. New York: Columbia University Press, 1943.

Chapter 2: Godfrey de Bouillon and the Early Knights Templar

The First Templars

Barber, Malcolm, and Keith Bate. *The Templars: Selected Sources*. Manchester, UK: Manchester University Press, 2002.

Baigent, Michael, Richard Leigh, and Henry Lincoln. *Holy Blood, Holy Grail*. New York: Delacorte Press, 1996.

Mackey, Albert. *Encyclopedia of Freemasonry*, Vol. 2. Whitefish, Mont.: Kessinger Publishing, 1991.

Murray, A. *Knights of the Holy Land: Crusader Kingdom of Jerusalem*. Jerusalem: The Israel Museum, 2000, p. 79.

Waite, Arthur. *The Brotherhood of the Rosy Cross*. New York: Barnes and Noble, 1993.

Godfrey de Bouillon's Templar Knights, Mount Sion, and the Essenes

Baigent, Michael, Richard Leigh, and Henry Lincoln. *Holy Blood, Holy Grail*. New York: Delacorte Press, 1996.

Haagensens, Erling, and Henry Lincoln. *The Templars' Secret Island*. Oxfordshire: Windrush Press, 2000.

Hallam, Elizabeth. *Chronicles of the Crusade*. New York: Welcome Rain, 2000.

Markale, Jean. *The Templar Treasure at Gisors*, Rochester, Vt.: Inner Traditions, 2003.

Pixner, B. "Church of the Apostles Found on Mount Sion." *Biblical Archaeology Review* (May/June 1990).

———. "Jerusalems Essene Gateway: Where the Community Lived in Jesus' Time." *Biblical Archaeology Review* (1997).

Selwood, Dominic. Knights of the Cloister: Templars and Hospitallers in Central Southern Occitania c. 1100–c.1300. New York: Boydell Press, 2002.

Chapter 3: The Ladies of the Grail
Salome: The Lady of the Grail

The Holy Bible: New International Version. London: Hodder and Stoughton, 1979.

The Legacy of Mary Magdelene

Barber, Malcolm. *The Trial of the Templars*. Cambridge: Cambridge University Press, 1993.

Pagels, Elaine. *The Gnostic Gospels*, New York: Vintage, London, 1989.

Picknett, Lynn. *Mary Magdalene: Christianity's Hidden Goddess*. New York: Carroll & Graf Publishers, 2003.

Picknett, Lynn, and Clive Prince. *The Templar Revelation: Secret Guardians of the True Identity of Christ*. New York: Touchstone, 1998.

Toresen, Karen Jo. *When Women Were Priests*. San Francisco: HarperSanFrancisco, 1995.

Che Knights Templar and Lady Wisdom

Barber, Richard. *The Knight and Chivalry*. New York: Boydell Press, 2000.

Begg, Ean. *The Cult of the Black Virgin*. New York: Penguin, 1985.

Haskins, Susan. *Mary Magdalene: Myth and Metaphor*. New York: Riverhead Trade, 1995.

Picknett, Lynn, and Clive Prince. *The Templar Revelation: Secret Guardians of the True Identity of Christ*. New York: Touchstone, 1998.

Ward, J. Upton. *The Rule of The Templars*. New York: Boydell Press, 1989.

Mary Magdalene: Mistress of the Grail

Broadhurst, Paul, and Hamish Miller. *Dance of the Dragon*. York: Pendragon Partnership, 2000.

Hafiz. *The Gift*. Trans. Daniel Ladinsky. New York: Penguin, 1999.

Kidd, Sue Monk. *The Secret Life of Bees*. New York: Penguin, 2003.

Pagels, Elaine, interviewed for "Jesus, Mary, and Da Vinci." *ABC Primetime*, ABC, November 3, 2003.

Van Biema, David. "Mary Magdalene—Saint or Sinner." *Time*. 11 August 2003.

Starbird, Margaret. *The Goddess in the Gospels*. Rochester, Vt.: Bear & Company, 1998.

Chapter 4: The Templar and Related Mysteries

Abbot Henry de Blois, Templars, and the Holy Grail

Carley, James P. *Glastonbury Abbey*. New York: Boydell Press, 1988.

Glaston, John de. *The Chronicle of Glastonbury Abbey*. New York: Boydell Press, 2001.

Jenkins, Elizabeth. *The Mystery of King Arthur*. London: Joseph, 1975.

Laidler, Keith. *The Head of God*. London: Weidenfeld and Nicolson, 1998.

Maltwood, Katharine. *Guide to Glastonbury's Temple of the Stars*. Cambridge: J. Clark, 1964.

Matthews, D. *King Stephen*. London: Habledon and London, 2002.

Michell, John. *New Light on the Ancient Mysteries of Glastonbury*. Glastonbury: Gothic Image Publications, 1991.

Riall, N. *Henry de Blois, Bishop of Winchester—A Patron of the Twelfth-Century Renaissance*, Vol. V. Hampshire County Council, 1994.

Scott, John. *The Early History of Glastonbury: An Edition, Translation and Study of William of Malmesbury's De Antiquitate Glastonie Ecclesie*. New York: Boydell Press, 2001.

Weir, Alison. *Eleanor of Aquitaine: A Life*. New York: Ballantine Books, 2001.

Winchester Cathedral (Pitkin Guide). Hampshire: Jarrold Publishing, 1998.

Abraxas: The Seal of the Inner Order Templars?

Barber, Malcolm. *The Trial of the Templars*. Cambridge: Cambridge University Press, 1993.

Becker Udo, Ed. *The Continuum Encyclopedia of Symbols*. Trans. Lance W. Garmer, New York: Continuum International Publishing, 1992.

Drury, Nevil. and S. Skinner. *The Search for Abraxas*. Lincoln: Spearman, 1972.

Holroyd, Stuart. *The Elements of Gnosticism*. Dorset: Element Books, 1994.

Partner, P. *The Murdered Magicians*. Oxford: Oxford University Press, 1981.

Room, Adrian, Ed. *Brewer's Dictionary of Phrases and Fables*. Oxford: Oxford University Press, 2000.

Segal, R. *The Gnostic Jung*. Princeton: Princeton University Press, 1992.

Knights Templar House, Kelvedon, Essex

Hamilton, Andrew. *The Lion Inn, Kelvedon*. (c. 1890).

Kentish, Basil. *Kelvedon and Its Antiquities*. West Sussex: Phillimore, 1974.

Gardner, Laurence. *Bloodline of the Holy Grail*. Glouchester, Mass.: Fair Winds Press, 2004.

Simon, Edith. *The Piebald Standard*. Brooklyn: AMS Press, 1977.

Wright, Thomas. *The History and Topography of the County of Essex*. G. Virtue Publishing, 1842.

The Templars of Rousillon

Hammott, Ben. "Saunieres Treasure Tomb." *Journal of the Rennes Alchemist* (October, 2003).

Littleton, C. *From Scythia to Camelot.* New York: Garland, 2000.

Mazeires, M. Society of Arts and Sciences of Carcassonne, Tome III, 4th Series. (1984).

Wallace-Hadrill, J.M. *Long-Haired Kings and Other Studies in Frankish History.* Toronto: University of Toronto Press, 1982.

Wolfram, Herwig. *The History of the Goths.* Berkeley: University of California Press, 1990.

Schiehallion: Mount Zion in the Far North

The Holy Bible: Revised Standard Version. Oxford: Oxford University Press, 2002.

Were the Templars Head Worshippers?

Barber, Malcolm. *The Trial of the Templars.* Cambridge: Cambridge University Press, 1993.

Schonfield, Hugh. *The Essene Odyssey.* Dorset: Element Books, 1993.

Nicholson, H. *The Knights Templar—a New History.* Gloucestershire: Sutton Publishing, 2001.

Coulton, G. C., *Five Centuries of Religion.* London: Octagon Books, 1979, pp. 93–93.

Chapter 5: Templar Preceptories

Balantradock: The Scottish Temple

Baigent, Michael, and Richard Leigh. *The Temple and the Lodge.* New York: Arcade Publishing, 1991.

Begg, Deike and Ean. *In Search of the Holy Grail and the Precious Blood.* New York: Thorsons Publishing, 1995.

Edwards, John. "The Knights Templars in Scotland." Transactions of the Scottish Ecclesiological Society, 1913.

Gardner, Laurence. *Bloodline of the Holy Grail.* Glouchester, Mass.: Fair Winds Press, 2004.

Gorebridge *Yesterdays: The 1983 Yearbook of Gorebridge and District Local History Society.* N.p.: n.d.

Johnstone, Iain. *Temple Old Parish Church*. N.p., n.d.

Liddell, Eric. *An Abstract History: Knights Templar and Freemasons in Scotland*. N.p., n.d.

MacGibbon, Ross. *The Ecclesiastical Architecture of Scotland*. Vol. 2. Edinburgh: Mercat Press, 1995.

Midlothian. *An Illustrated Architectural Guide*. N.p.: 1995.

Proceedings of the Society of Antiquaries. "Temple, Midlothian." N.p.: 1911/1912.

"Royal Commission on the Ancient Historical Monuments of Scotland." N.p.: 1929.

"The Knights Templar in Scotland." *The Scottish Review*. N.p.: 1898.

Vernon, Stephen. "Temple." *Cockpen Bazaar Book*. October, 1897.

St. Michael's Church, Garway

Barber, Malcolm. *The Trial of the Templars*. Cambridge: Cambridge University Press, 1993.

Tapper, A. *A Brief History of Christianity 500 A.D.–2000 A.D.* N.p., n.d.

Tull, George. *Traces of the Templars*. Rotherham: The King's England Press, 2000.

Yates, J. F. *The Church of St. Michael*, Garway. N.p., n.d.

Chapter 6: Freemasonry
A History of Canadian Masonic Templarism

Dafoe, Stephen. "Masonic Templarism." *Http://www.templarhistory.com/masonic.html*.

Dafoe, Stephen. "Masonic Templarism in Canada: An Interview With the Grand Historian." *Templar History Magazine*. Vol. 1. N.p., n.d.

Dafoe, Stephen. "The Shriners: the Ancient Arabic Order of the Nobles of the Mystic Shrine." *Http://www.thelodgeroom.com/shrine.html*.

Kaulback, Michael. "The First Knights Templar in the United States." *http://www.guigue.org/guitex28.htm*.

Sovereign Great Priory of Canada. *Christian Chivalry and Freemasonry*. N.p., n.d.

Sovereign Great Priory of Canada. "Annual Proceedings." N.p.: 1967.

Sovereign Great Priory of Canada. "Annual Proceedings." N.p.: 1984.

Sovereign Great Priory of Canada. "Annual Proceedings." N.p.: 1991.

Sovereign Great Priory of Canada. "Annual Proceedings." N.p.: 1998.

Sovereign Great Priory of Canada. "Annual Proceedings." N.p.: 1999.

Sovereign Great Priory of Canada. "Annual Proceedings." N.p.: 2000.

Sovereign Great Priory of Canada. "Annual Proceedings." N.p.: 2001.

Ramsay Oration. N.p., n.d.

United Grand Lodge of England. *Articles of Union*. N.p.: 1813.

The Early History of Freemasonry

Calendar of State Papers Relating to Scotland, 1581-1583, Vol. 13. London: n.p., 1910.

Edwards. G.P. "William Elphinstone: His College Chapel and the Second of April." *Aberdeen University Review*, 1i 1985) p. 1–17.

Grand Lodge of Antient Free and Accepted Masons of Scotland. *Historical Sketch of the Grand Lodge of Antient Free and Accepted Masons of Scotland*. N.p.: 1986.

Hey, R.A. *Genealogie of the Saintclaires of Rosslyn, Including the Chartulary of Rosslyn*. N.p.: 1835.

Hibbert, Christopher. *Charles I.*, London: Weidenfeld and Nicholson, 1968.

Kirk, J., Ed. *The Records of the Synod of Lothian and Tweeddale* 1589-96. Edinburgh: Stair Society, 1977.

McMillan, William. *The Worship of the Reformed Church of Scotland 1550–1638*. London: James Clarke and Company, 1931.

Paton, H. M., Ed. *Accounts of the Masters of Works, 1556–67*. Edinburgh: n.p., 1957.

Preston, William. *Illustrations of Freemasonry*. London: n.p., 1746.

Robinson, Cyril E. *A History of England, 1485–1688*. London: Methuen, 1920.

Somerville, John. *Memorie of the Somervilles; Being a History of the Baronial House of Somerville,* ed. Sir Walter Scott. Edinburgh: n.p., 1815.

Stevenson, David. *The Origins of Freemasonry*. Cambridge: Cambridge University Press, 1990.

Wright, Dudley, Ed. *Gould's History of Freemasonry*, Vol. III. London: Caxton, 1890.

Index

About the Authors

STEPHEN DAFOE is the author of *Everything I Need to Know About Freemasonry* (Templar Books, 2004), and *Unholy Worship* (Templar Books, 1998). In addition, he is the coauthor of *The Templar Continuum* (Templar Books, 2000) and *Warriors and Bankers* (Templar Books, 1999), both of which were written with Alan Butler.

BARRY DUNFORD is the author of several acclaimed articles, and the book *The Holy Land of Scotland: Jesus in Scotland and the Gospel of the Grail, Sacred Connections* (Highland Perthshire, 2002).

SANDY HAMBLETT is the editor and publisher of the *Journal of the Rennes Alchemist*.

YURI LEITCH is a artist and writer based in Glastonbury, England. (View artwork at *http://uk.geocities.com/yuri.leitch@btinternet.com*)

ROBERT LOMAS is the author of *Turning the Hiram Key* (Fair Winds Press, 2005), *The Invisible College* (Headline Book Publishing, 2003), and

The Man Who Invented the Twentieth Century (Headline Book Publishing, 1999), and the coauthor of numerous other titles.

BOB MANDER is a writer and researcher based in Liverpool, England.

MARK McGIVERON is a researcher and writer based in Glastonbury, England.

ODDVAR OLSEN cofounded *The Temple* in August 2002. Since then he has edited and published eight issues of this very successful publication. He has also written several articles for magazines in the United Kingdom and abroad. In 2005, Olsen hosted the The Temple Conferences, which was a series of lectures focused on the Templar legacy.

LYNN PICKNETT is the author of *Mary Magdalene—Christianity's Hidden Goddess* (Carroll and Graf Publishers, 2003). In addition, she coauthored (with Clive Price) *The Stargate Conspiracy* (Little, Brown, 1999), *The Templar Revelation: Secret Guardians of the True Identity of Christ* (Bantham Press, 1997), and *Turin Shroud: In Whose Image?* (Bloomsbury, 1994).

DAMIAN PRESTBURY is a writer and researcher based in Manchester, England.

ANI WILLIAMS is a musician, writer, and tour operator based in Sedona, Arizona. Learn more at *www.aniwilliams.com*.

TERENCE WILSON first published his article, "Knights Templar House, Kelevdon—Essex," in issue four of *The Temple*.

VINCENT ZUBRAS is the Grand Master of the OPCCTS. He first published his article "The Larmenius Charter and the Legitimacy of Modern-Day Knights Templar," in issue three of *The Temple*.

EXPECT SOMETHING DIFFERENT
FROM NEW PAGE BOOKS

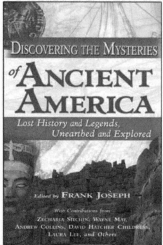

**Discovering the Mysteries
of Ancient America**
Lost History and Legends,
Unearthed and Explored
Frank Joseph, et. al.
1-56414-842-4

Celtic Myth and Legend
Revised Edition
Charles Squire
1-56414-534-4

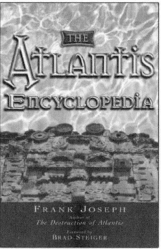

The Mysteries of Druidry
Celtic Mysticism, Theory & Practice
Brendan Myers, Ph.D.
1-56414-878-5

The Atlantis Encyclopedia
Frank Joseph
1-56414-795-9

Visit NewPageBooks.com for our latest Catalogs or
call 1-800-227-3371 to place an order